11/08

DISCARD

LOSING MATT SHEPARD

Losing Matt Shepard

LIFE AND POLITICS IN
THE AFTERMATH OF
ANTI-GAY MURDER

Beth Loffreda

COLUMBIA UNIVERSITY PRESS   NEW YORK

Columbia University Press

Publishers Since 1893

New York   Chichester, West Sussex

Copyright © 2000 Beth Loffreda

Library of Congress Cataloging-in-Publication Data

Loffreda, Beth.

Losing Matt Shepard : life and politics in the
aftermath of anti-gay murder / Beth Loffreda.

p. cm.

Includes bibliographical references.

ISBN 0–231–11858–9 (cloth : alk. paper)

1. Shepard, Matthew, d. 1998—Death and burial.

2. Gay men—Crimes against—Wyoming—Laramie.

3. Homicide—Wyoming—Laramie.

4. Homophobia—Wyoming—Laramie.

5. Laramie (Wyo.)—Social conditions.

I. Title.

HV6250.4.H66 L63 2000

306.76′6′0978795—dc21   00-043172

♾

Casebound editions of
Columbia University Press books
are printed on permanent and
durable acid-free paper.

Printed in the United States of America

Designed by Audrey Smith

c 10 9 8 7 6 5 4 3 2 1

For Tripp and Joe

Contents .

Preface

On the night of October 6th, 1998, Matt Shepard, a twenty-one-year-old gay University of Wyoming student, stopped in at the Fireside Bar in downtown Laramie for a drink. A day later, in the early evening of Wednesday, October 7th, a mountain biker found Matt lashed to a fence on the outskirts of town, beaten, pistol-whipped, unconscious, and barely breathing. Matt never regained consciousness, and he died five days later, in the early hours of Monday, October 12th. His killers—Aaron McKinney and Russell Henderson, Laramie men in their early twenties like Matt—were already in custody.

These meager facts are one way to tell the story of those few days. But other stories began to take shape during that cruel stretch, as Matt lay in a Colorado hospital, his doctors struggling to save him, his parents traveling to be at his side. Even before

Matt died, he underwent a strange, American transubstantiation, seized, filtered, and fixed as an icon by a national news media dedicated to swift and consumable tragedy and by a national politics convulsed by gay rights. For most of the nation, Matt Shepard has become a metaphor in the glow of computer screens and television sets. He has taken up permanent electronic residence there, and a few bits of Laramie—the fence he was tied to, the bar he left, the "cowboy culture" that some say killed him—have traveled there with him. But such media alchemies leave much behind: the raw and inchoate stuff that resists easy telling, that lacks clear beginnings and resonant endings, the stuff of daily life before and after such crystallizing events.

This book tries to take the measure of daily life since October 1998 in Laramie—a complicated town of roughly 26,000 in a rural, poor, and conservative state, a town haunted by Matt's death. Taking such measure is no easy task, for while journalists, politicians, critics, and writers might make a living talking about "America"—as if it exists, as if it coheres, as if it has transparency and intention—Laramie might not be so easy to see. Laramie is no thesis, although it has been treated as such in the months since Matt's death; Laramie is no diagnosis, no explanation for murder. Laramie can't offer the final answer for why Matt died. Laramie didn't kill Matt, but Laramie didn't make much room for him either, before he was murdered. What Laramie might do instead, in its drifting and reversing textures, is let us see a few things. It might let us see how the politics of sexuality—perhaps now the most divisive issue in America's "culture wars"—plays out in a forgotten corner of the country, and how homophobia works not just through the viciousness of physical violence but also through the daily erosion of selfhood by the friction of widespread, casually expressed hatred. It might let us see how, in the post–civil rights era, so many of us have substituted empathy for activism. It might let us see the unpredicted transformations and generosities that so many individuals here experienced, and let us see the stands they took as they grappled with what such events demanded of them. And it might let us ask not simply why Matt's death haunts so many of us now, but why it should.

I moved to Laramie just a few months before Matt was killed. I write this book as a University of Wyoming professor new to the state and in love with the place and as a straight woman and faculty adviser to the campus Lesbian Gay Bisexual Transgender Association—in other words, as both an insider and outsider to these events. What follows draws on my observations, local newspaper accounts, and dozens of interviews with students, townspeople, state politicians, activists, and gay and lesbian residents. I don't pretend that this book is comprehensive, that it can or will represent every townsperson's reaction to Matt's death, every perspective on homosexuality and homophobia. I doubt if such a task is possible, and I'm not interested in its easier substitutes, in the blank-eyed surfaces of statistical surveys ("Do you support homosexuality? Yes or no.") or the textureless generalizations of much rapid-response cultural criticism ("They've got a bar called the Cowboy? Well, that tells you pretty much all you need to know."). I've tried to capture what I've found to be the typical responses to Matt's death, but I'm also interested in recounting the atypical, the surprising, the stories and viewpoints that most people, inside or outside Wyoming, don't expect to find here: from the ranch son who now runs a cowboy fetish and phone sex business, to the high school dropout who has become an antiviolence activist.

Nor will this book dig into the biographical complexities and vulnerabilities of Matt's own life or the lives of his killers. I want to leave Matt Shepard's privacy intact, and while such biographical undertakings are potentially worthy tasks, they don't necessarily get us very far in understanding the places undergirding such events or in understanding why this case, among so many other brutal anti-gay murders, gripped the nation so fiercely. This book investigates those larger questions from a local perspective. It documents some of the significant things that happened in Laramie after Matt's death—the upwelling of genuine grief and self-questioning, the vigils, the concerts, the trials, the protests—and some of the significant things that didn't happen—a state bias crimes law, for example. And it records individual voices mostly unheard in the media frenzy that followed the murder.

Crucial to that last task is the year and a half of conversations

I've had with gay men and lesbians in Laramie. Invariably, when I've told someone from outside Wyoming—a journalist, an activist, an acquaintance—that I'm writing about gay and lesbian lives here, they've responded with something like this: "Huh. I didn't know there were any" (a sentiment shared by plenty of individuals inside Wyoming as well). Of course, there are—those lives may be hard won, but they're won all the same, and the strangest gap in the media attention to the murder has been the widespread failure to ask local gays and lesbians what they make of it. I've interviewed members of the United Gays and Lesbians of Wyoming and the university's Lesbian Gay Bisexual Transgender Association, but I've also sought out men and women who have found their partners, vocations, and pleasures outside those organized networks. In academic and popular culture both, we rarely pay much heed to rural lives, and to rural minorities even less; if this book makes any contribution, what I hope most is that it acknowledges the density and richness of lives typically seen as unrelievedly victimized, impossibly unsatisfactory, or simply nonexistent.

I hope too that this book does justice to Laramie. What "justice" means, of course, is up for grabs: I've spoken to some who want Laramie sentenced and condemned as a hateful place; some who want Laramie defended, who feel deeply that the good of this town far outshines the bad; and some who simply want the murder, and all that swirls around it, forgotten. Representatives of each of those sensibilities draw breath in this book, and I myself have worn a path between the first two, as I've found myself alternately persuaded by those who truly love this place and those who long to flee it. It's a whiplash condition, perhaps because Laramie itself has been whiplashed in the past year, its residents confronting a startling ugliness, watching themselves on television, trying to reconcile what they thought with what they now were forced to know. If anything has come close to uniting Laramie since October 1998, it is that condition of whiplash. There's no cure for it—certainly not forgetfulness— and instead I've come to see the whiplash as an opportunity, a chance to see the stubborn incommensurabilities, the halfway covenants, and the halting transformations of Laramie in the aftermath of Matt Shepard's murder.

This book, as it seeks to portray those things, meanders a bit: it would be a lie to say there's an easy story to tell about Laramie since the murder, if by "story" you meant a tidy narrative with a steady propulsion and one direction, protagonists and antagonists, characters working in rhythmic concert or stark opposition toward an inevitable resolution. It's a cliché of the postmodern era to point out the dishonesty of grand narratives or the corrosion of truth claims; my point, a lot less ambitious, is simply that it's hard to know both what happened that night at the fence and what happened later. It's even harder to know where the story you could tell about Laramie should end. You could say the climax of Laramie's story happened in the courtrooms where the killers encountered their punishments; you could say the real ending unraveled in city halls and state legislative offices, in the life and death of ordinances, laws, and resolutions; you could say the matter concluded in the expansions and contractions of the hearts of ordinary people. In the chapters that follow, I've tried to track the repercussions of Matt's murder through each of those places, by talking to some of the people who, though mostly unacquainted with Matt when he was alive, nevertheless felt those repercussions, and felt them hard, after he was gone.

Chapter One describes Laramie in the October of Matt's death—the rush of protests and memorials, the arraignments of the killers, the arrival of the media, and the stunning transformation of Matthew into martyr, fueled by a surreal mixture of heartfelt identification, opportunistic politicking, and factual error. In an instant that October, Laramie unwillingly arrived at the center of national debates about bias, violence, and their legal remedies; and Wyoming, generally laconic and frequently defensive when it came to talking about inequality and sexuality both, found itself in some difficult conversations.

Chapters Two and Three take some time to look at what we in Wyoming didn't always want to talk about. Chapter Two considers the political debates about bias crimes legislation that confronted Wyoming in the months that followed the murder, as well as the unevenness of equality, the troubles of race and class, in Laramie itself. Chapter Three looks in particular at gay and lesbian life and politics in Wyoming, both before and after that October, arguing that while Wyoming is neither particularly worse nor particularly better than the rest of America when it comes to anti-gay sentiments, gay life here nevertheless has a uniqueness that shouldn't be overlooked.

The remainder of the book returns to the many ways Laramie has tried to respond to the loss of Matt Shepard. Chapter Four discusses the spring and summer after the murder, when visitors like Elton John and Fred Phelps came to town, some local activists found their callings, and Russell Henderson, the first of the killers to come before the court, was sentenced. Chapter Five discusses the first anniversary of Matt's death, a week in which the second round of memorial events and the trial of Aaron McKinney both fell. Returning to October returns the book to the murder itself, to the elusiveness of that night, to the difficulty of knowing exactly what we mean when we say Matt died because he was gay.

Chapter Six looks at a few days in April 2000. As thousands of gay men and lesbians marched on Washington in an event replete with corporate backers and celebrity cheerleaders, back in Wyoming, in Matt's hometown of Casper, a new local anti-gay organization held its first public presentation. That same weekend, a small group of pro-gay grassroots activists gathered in the same town, far from the celebratory satisfactions of the Washington march. And four days later, the Laramie City Council cast the deciding vote on the bias crimes ordinance it had spent more than a year trying to dodge. If those few days are an end to this book, it's not because they're the end to the story. But they are close to a summation—to a capturing of the daily contradictoriness, the willed and porous amnesias, the tense compromises, the new and deep personal commitments, and the unfinished clash of politics that are Laramie's necessary inheritance.

Author's Note

Much of this book is based on interviews I have conducted with residents of Laramie and of Wyoming in general. I have used the full names of public figures—journalists, state and local politicians, and Laramie residents repeatedly portrayed in the national media. When given permission by interviewees, I have also used the full names of private citizens. Some of my interview subjects have asked that I identify them only by first name, to protect their privacy, which I have agreed to do. In the case of three interviewees, I have agreed to use pseudonyms; each pseudonym is noted in the text.

LOSING MATT SHEPARD

CHAPTER ONE

Perhaps the first thing to know about Laramie, Wyoming, is that it is beautiful. On most days the high-altitude light is so precise and clear that Laramie appears some rarefied place without need of an atmosphere. We were having a stretch of days like that in early October 1998, as the news began to trickle in that a man had been found beaten somewhere on the edge of town. We'd later sort out the key facts: that Matt Shepard had encountered Russell Henderson and Aaron McKinney late Tuesday night in the Fireside Bar; that he'd left with them; that they had driven him in a pickup truck to the edge of town; that Henderson had tied him to a fence there and McKinney had beaten him viciously and repeatedly with a .357 Magnum; that they had taken his shoes and wallet and intended to rob his apartment but instead returned to town and got into a fight with two other young men, Jeremy Herrera and Emiliano Morales (McKinney clubbed Morales on the head with the same gun, still covered in Matt's blood; Herrera retaliated by striking McKinney's head with a heavy stick); that the police, responding to the altercation, picked up Henderson—McKinney had fled—and saw the gun, Matt's credit card, and his shoes in the truck but didn't yet know the fatal meaning of those objects; that after being released later that night, Henderson and his girlfriend, Chasity Pasley, and McKinney and his girlfriend, Kristen Price, began to hatch their false alibis; and that through all this Matt remained tied to the fence and wouldn't be found until Wednesday evening, after an entire night and most of a day had passed. We'd learn all that, and learn that Matt's sexuality was woven through all of it. Those facts reached us swiftly, but making sense of them took much longer.

Jim Osborn, a recent graduate of the university's education program, was the chair of the Lesbian Gay Bisexual Transgender Association that October, a group that Matt, a freshman, had just recently joined. The LGBTA is the sole gay organization on campus and in Laramie itself. While students make up most of its membership, it welcomes university staff and townspeople as well, although only a few have joined. The group has been active since 1990; before that, another gay campus organization, Gays and Lesbians of Wyoming—GLOW—had an intermittent but vivid life in the 1970s and early 1980s. Women typically outnumber men at LGBTA meetings, although not by a significant margin; altogether, attendance on any given night usually hovers between ten and twenty members. The group's email list, however, reaches far more. There's no single reason for that discrepancy; it most likely arises from a combination of factors, including the familiar reluctance of many college students to join groups and, more specifically in this case, the anxiety some gay or questioning students might feel attending a public meeting.

The LGBTA gathers weekly in a nondescript, carpeted seminar room on the second floor of the university union. It has no office space of its own. (When hundreds of letters arrived after Matt's murder, the group stored them in the corner of the Multicultural Resource Center downstairs.) Meetings are usually hourlong sessions, punctuated by bursts of laughter, during which the group plans upcoming events—speakers, dances, potlucks. The LGBTA juggles numerous, sometimes contradictory roles as it tries to be a public face for gay and lesbian issues on campus (organizing events, running panels about sexuality for many courses) and at the same time create a comfortable, safe space for socializing in a town without a gay bar or bookstore. It also serves as something of a gay news exchange, sharing information about what teachers might be supportive or not, what places in town and elsewhere might be safe or not, what's happening that might not show up in the campus paper, *The Branding Iron*.

That last role mattered on Tuesday, October 6th. As the members handled the last-minute details of Gay Awareness Week, scheduled to begin the following Monday, Jim Osborn warned the group to be careful. The week before, he had been harassed while walking across campus. A young man—Jim thinks he was probably a university student—had come up behind him, said, "You're one of those faggots, aren't you?" and thrown a punch. Jim is a big, strapping white man from northern Wyoming; he blocked the punch and hit his attacker. They then took off in opposite directions. Jim didn't report the attack to the police but did want to alert members of the LGBTA that it had happened. Matt was among those there to hear Jim's story. After the meeting, members of the group, including Matt and Jim, went out for coffee at the College Inn, something of a Tuesday-night LGBTA tradition. Jim remembers that Matt sat at the other end of a crowded table. It was the last Jim would see of him.

Jim can talk an eloquent blue streak and is something of an organizational genius—at LGBTA meetings I've listened to him recall the minutiae of university regulations and budget protocols as if they were fond personal memories. He also has a staggeringly large network of friends and acquaintances. On Thursday morning, he got an email from Tina Labrie, a friend of his and Matt's; she had introduced them in August, when Matt, new to Laramie, wanted to learn about the LGBTA. The message said that Matt had been found near death the evening before and was hospitalized in Fort Collins, Colorado. (Matt had initially been taken to Ivinson

Memorial Hospital in Laramie and was then transferred to Poudre Valley Hospital's more sophisticated trauma unit. While Matt was being treated in the Ivinson Memorial ER, McKinney was a few curtains down, admitted earlier for the head wound he had received from Herrera; like Matt, McKinney would also be transferred to Poudre Valley.) Horrified, Jim phoned Tina and learned that the police were trying to reconstruct Matt's whereabouts on Tuesday evening. When he called the Laramie Police to tell them what he knew, an officer informed him that Matt wasn't going to make it. Matt was suffering from hypothermia, and there was severe trauma to the brain stem. The officer told Jim that one side of Matt's head had been beaten in several inches and that the neurosurgeon was quite frankly surprised that he was still alive.

Bob Beck, news director for Wyoming Public Radio, also got word of the attack on Thursday. Beck has lived in Laramie since 1984; he's a tall, lanky midwesterner with a serious jones for Chicago Bulls basketball. On the radio he speaks in the sedated tones cultivated by NPR reporters everywhere, but in person he displays a vinegary wit and a likably aggravated demeanor. "It was a strange thing," he told me. "I teach a class, and one of my students called up and told me he needed to miss class that day because one of his friends had got beaten up very badly and was taken to the hospital in Fort Collins." That student was Phil Labrie, Tina's husband. Worried when they couldn't reach Matt, they had called the police on Wednesday, shortly after Matt was found, and learned what had happened. "[Phil] didn't tell me a lot of details because he said the cops had told him not to really tell anyone. But then he said I will know about it later and it will be a big story. . . . So I right away thought I better follow up on this immediately." He contacted the Albany County Sheriff's Office and learned that a press conference would be held later that day.

Beck attended the press conference that day—typically a routine exercise, but one that in this case would unexpectedly and profoundly shape public reaction to the attack. According to Beck, the sheriff

Chapter One

indicated that there was a young man who had been very badly beaten, was on life support, had been taken to Poudre Valley Hospital. During the questioning, the sheriff at the time, Gary Puls, indicated that they thought he may have been beaten because he was gay. And when he described this situation to us he told us that [Shepard] was found by a mountain bike rider, tied to a fence like a scarecrow. My recollection is there was discussion of exactly what do you mean, "tied like a scarecrow," and I think every single one of us who were in the room got the impression certainly of being tied up spread-eagled, splayed out.

Matt hadn't actually been tied like a scarecrow; when he was approached first by the mountain biker, Aaron Kreifels, and then by Reggie Fluty, the sheriff's deputy who answered Kreifels's emergency call, Matt lay on his back, head propped against the fence, legs outstretched. His hands were lashed behind him and tied barely four inches off the ground to a fencepost. In dramatic and widely reported testimony, Fluty would later state that at first she thought Matt could have been no older than thirteen, he was so small (Matt was only five feet two inches, barely over one hundred pounds). And when she described Matt's brutally disfigured face, she said that the only spots not covered in blood were the tracks cleansed by his tears—an enduring image that continues to appear in essays, poetry, and songs dedicated to Shepard. It is most likely that Kreifels was the source of Puls's press-conference description. Kreifels told police and reporters that he at first thought Matt was a scarecrow flopped on the ground, maybe some kind of Halloween joke staged a few weeks early. No matter its provenance, the notion that Matt had been strung up in something akin to a crucifixion became the starting point for the reporting and reaction to come.

Beck says, "I know that's how we all reported it, and that was never corrected."* The vicious symbolism of that image, combined

---

* Melanie Thernstrom's essay on the murder in the March 1999 issue of *Vanity Fair* notes that Matt was not strung up, but only in a parenthetical remark near the end of the piece, and the article itself has the title "The Crucifixion of Matthew Shepard." JoAnn Wypijewski's tough-minded essay "A Boy's Life,"

with Puls's early acknowledgment that the beating might have been an anti-gay hate crime, drew instant attention. Attending the press conference were the Associated Press, members of the Wyoming and Colorado media, Beck, and two friends of Matt, Walt Boulden and Alex Trout. According to press reports, Boulden and Trout, afraid that the attack might go unnoticed, had already begun to alert the media earlier that day. Boulden had had plans with Matt for Tuesday night; Matt had canceled and later, apparently, had decided to head off to the Fireside alone. Boulden was not shy about seizing the attack as a political opportunity, linking the assault to the Wyoming legislature's failure to pass a hate crimes bill: he told reporters that "they said nothing like that happens in Wyoming because someone is gay, but we've always known some-one would have to get killed or beaten before they finally listened. I just can't believe it happened to someone I cared so much about." By Friday morning, when the police already had McKinney, Hen-derson, Price, and Pasley in custody (Beck says "the investigation was one of the better I've seen"), the media interest, spurred by Thursday's press conference, had increased exponentially.

At the same time, Laramie's gay residents were learning what had happened. Stephanie and Lisa, a lesbian couple active in the LGBTA, heard the news from Jim on Thursday evening. Lisa, a striking redhead and a good friend of Jim's, talked to him first: "He told me Matt had been beaten. And I said, well, shit, how badly? Is he okay? And Jim said no—he's in critical condition, had to be airlifted to Poudre Valley." Both Stephanie and Lisa knew Matt only slightly, although Stephanie had expected to have the chance to grow closer. She had just agreed to be Matt's mentor in a pro-gram the LGBTA was considering as a way to welcome new students to the gay community. Like Lisa, Steph has an edgy, witty charisma, but it deserted her that night, as she, Lisa, and Jim

---

which appeared in the September 1999 issue of *Harper's Magazine*, was the first thorough demystification of this myth in the national media, but many people still believe it. For example, Melissa Etheridge's song "Scarecrow" on her 1999 album *Breakdown* relies on it, as well as on other early misstatements of fact, including the false report that Shepard had been burned by his killers.

watched the first TV news reports. "There was this horrifying feeling that we were standing on the brink of learning something really, really awful," she says of that Thursday. "Like the part in the horror movie just before she opens the closet and finds the dead cat. It was that moment. For a day. And then we got the facts . . . and everything started happening at this tremendous speed. The next day was the day the story broke. And there were newspaper reporters and cameras all over the place." Steph had called me early that Friday morning, spreading word of the attack and warning people associated with the LGBTA to watch their backs: "I can remember wanting to tell everybody, absolutely everybody, wanting to physically grab people by their lapels and make them listen."

An atmosphere of genuine shock permeated the university; most students and faculty I encountered that day wore stunned and distraught expressions that I imagine mirrored my own; they seemed absorbed simply in trying to understand how something so brutal could have happened within a short walk of their daily lives. Gay and lesbian members of the university that I spoke to felt a wrenching mix of fear and sadness; many, including Stephanie and Lisa, were also immediately and intensely angry. A number of students in my morning American Literature course, after a long discussion in which they sought answers for how to publicly express their repugnance for the crime, decided that the university's homecoming parade, coincidentally scheduled for the following morning, would be an ideal site for that response. Finding like-minded students in the United Multicultural Council, the LGBTA, and the student government, they began printing flyers, making hundreds of armbands, and arranging permits to join the parade.* Their unjaded

---

*While the United Multicultural Council did good work that day, and while some strong connections have been made between the UMC and the LGBTA since Matt's death, it would be wrong to imply that those ties have been built without friction. Carina Evans, a university student who worked in the Minority Affairs Office that year, observed that at the time some members of the "diversity clubs" represented by the UMC "would not deal with the gay issue. The United Multicultural Council had no representation from the LGBTA, had no representation of openly gay students—and I think that's not at all multicultural. But they don't want to handle that. It's not like they're hostile about it,

eagerness to publicly involve themselves in the case contrasted sharply with the university administration's first official response, much of which had concerned itself with pointing out that the attack happened off campus and was committed by nonstudents.

On Friday afternoon—as Jim Osborn began to field what would eventually become an overwhelming flood of media requests for interviews—the four accused appeared in court for the first time. Bob Beck attended the initial appearance: "That's where you bring in the people, read them formal charges, and we then get their names, backgrounds—which is important for us." Beck had left for the courthouse a half hour early; initial appearances are typically held in a small room in the courthouse basement, and Beck thought it might be more full than usual. He was right. "It was sold out. It was wall-to-wall cameras." Residents of Laramie—professors and LGBTA members in particular—had also come to witness the proceedings. So many attended that the reading of the charges had to be delayed while everyone moved upstairs to the much larger district court. Beck remembers, "I went in—in fact it was so crowded I got shoved by where the jury box is located—and I stood behind the defendants when they came in. I got a really good look at everybody, and I was actually surprised at how young they looked, how scared they looked, and how little they were." Only Henderson, McKinney, and Chasity Pasley were charged that day; separate proceedings had been arranged for Kristen Price. Pasley wept throughout. She was someone Jim Osborn knew well and liked. She worked in the campus activities center and had helped Jim countless times when the LGBTA needed photocopying or assistance setting up for an event. "She was very supportive of the group," Jim says. Often when he saw her on a Wednesday, she'd ask, "Hey, how'd it go last night?" In the past, he had seen her wearing one of the group's "Straight But Not Narrow" buttons.

I was in the courtroom that afternoon and can remember the

---

but they just don't encourage it." The tension flows both ways: Jay, a gay American Indian now active in the UMC, told me that some gay students of color he knows are uncomfortable attending LGBTA meetings because they feel that some members are not sensitive to racial differences.

professional flatness with which the county judge, Robert Castor, read the charges aloud. Castor had arrived in the courtroom to find a cameraman sitting at the prosecution's table, an early symbol of the persistent media invasion, Bob Beck believes, that frustrated the court and the prosecutor, Cal Rerucha, and led them to sharply limit information about the case thereafter. Castor charged McKinney and Henderson with three identical counts of kidnapping, aggravated robbery, and attempted first-degree murder; Pasley he charged with a count of accessory after the fact to attempted first-degree murder (in addition to providing false alibis for their boyfriends, she and Price had also helped dispose of evidence, including Henderson's bloody clothing). After each count, Castor recited "the essential facts" supporting the charge, in what became a truly grim ritual of repetition. In language I've condensed from the court documents, the essential facts were these: "On or between October 6, 1998, and the early morning hours of October 7, 1998, Aaron McKinney and Russell Henderson met Matthew Shepard at the Fireside Bar, and after Mr. Shepard confided he was gay, the subjects deceived Mr. Shepard into leaving with them in their vehicle to a remote area near Sherman Hills subdivision in Albany County. En route to said location, Mr. Shepard was struck in the head with a pistol." (McKinney, we'd later learn, had apparently told Matt, "We're not gay, and you just got jacked," before striking him.) "Upon arrival at said location, both subjects tied their victim to a buck fence, robbed him, and tortured him, while beating him with the butt of a pistol. During the incident, the victim was begging for his life. The subjects then left the area, leaving the victim for dead." By the third time Castor read that Matt had begged for his life, the courtroom had become choked with sickness and grief. The true darkness of the crime had become impossible to flee.

The next morning—Saturday—began with the university's homecoming parade. As the parade kicked off, one hundred students, university employees, and townspeople lined up at the end of the long string of floats and marching bands. They had quietly gathered in the morning chill to protest the attack on Matt. The leaders of the march carried a yellow banner painted with green circles, symbols of peace chosen by the UMC. They were followed by a silent crowd wearing matching armbands and holding signs that read "No Hate Crimes in Wyoming," "Is This What Equality Feels Like?" and "Straight But Not Stupid." I walked a few yards from the front, watching Carly Laucomer, a university student holding the middle of the banner, field questions from reporters walking backward a single pace in front of her. Beside me, Cat, another university student, muttered that she wished the marchers weren't so sparse. Cat, like Carly, was then a student in my American Literature course, a smart young woman usually prepared to be disappointed by the world around her. Laramie surprised her. As the march moved west down Ivinson Avenue, spectators began to join, walking off sidewalks into the street. By the time the march reached downtown (where a giant second-story banner proclaimed, "Hate Is Not a Wyoming Value") and circled back toward campus, it had swelled beyond even Cat's demanding expectations; final estimates ranged from five to eight hundred participants. It didn't seem like much—just a bunch of people quietly walking—but it was a genuinely spontaneous, grassroots effort to protest the attack and express the community's profound dismay, and in that sense it was unforgettable.

A very different sort of tribute to Matt appeared in the Colorado State University homecoming parade the same day in the city of Fort Collins. As Matt lay in the hospital just a few miles away, a float in the parade carried a scarecrow draped in anti-gay epithets. While the papers were reluctant to report the full range of insults, I heard that the signs read "I'm Gay" and "Up My Ass." Colorado State University acted quickly to punish the sorority and fraternity responsible for the float (the censured students blamed vandalism committed by an unknown third party), but still it is worth pausing for a moment to consider the degree of dehumanization such an act required, how much those responsible must have felt, however fleetingly or unconsciously, that Matt was not a fellow human being, their age, with his future torn away from him. Fort Collins is home to a visible and energetic community of gay activists, and the float was widely denounced. Still, a week later Fort Collins would vote down, by nearly a two-to-one margin, City Ordinance 22, a proposal to expand the city's antidiscrimination statute to include protections for gays and lesbians.

Later that Saturday, a moment of silence for Matt was held before the University of Wyoming's football game; players wore the UMC's symbols on their helmets. And, impossibly, the media presence continued to grow. Bob Beck, juggling requests for interviews with his own reporting, was in the thick of it and felt a growing frustration at the sloppiness of what he saw around him. "Right away it was horrible. Part of that, in fairness, was that we didn't have all the information we needed. While the sheriff was very up front at first, next thing you know, nobody's talking." City officials, naturally unprepared (in a town with barely a murder a year) for the onslaught, focused their resources on the investigation and, angry that Laramie was being depicted as a hate crimes capital, began to restrict press access. But the media, especially the TV tabloids, Beck says, needed to turn things around quickly, and since they were getting stonewalled by the city and by many Laramie residents, "it seemed like the place they went to interview everybody was in bars. As we all know who are in the media, if you want to get somebody to be very glib, give you a few quick takes, you want to go to a bar. And you certainly are going to meet a segment of our population that will have more interesting things to say." I remember watching for footage of the Saturday morning march later that evening and seeing instead precisely the sort of bar interview Beck describes, a quick and dirty media tactic I heard many residents mock in the coming months.

Beck also remembers one of the first television news reports he saw: "It was this woman reporter outside the Fireside doing what we call a bridge, a stand-up: 'Hate: it's a common word in Wyoming.'" Beck couldn't believe it, but that mirrored precisely the assumptions of most of the media representatives he encountered that week. Journalists who interviewed him began with comments like, "Well, this kind of thing probably happens a lot up there," or, "You have that cowboy mentality in Wyoming, so this was bound to happen." Reporters criticized Laramie, he says, for not having a head trauma unit, not having gay bars, not pushing back homecoming. The tone of the questioning was hostile; Jim Osborn, speaking to journalists from locations as far-flung as Australia and the Netherlands, encountered it too. Jim says the press he spoke to wanted to hear that this was a hateful, redneck town, that Wyoming was, in the inane rhyming of some commentators, "the hate state." But Jim insisted on what he considered accurate: "Nobody expects murder here—nobody. This is not a place where you kill your neighbor, and we see each other as neighbors. This is a good place."

But the crime, and Laramie, had already begun to take on a second life, a broadcast existence barely tethered to the truths of that night or this place, an existence nourished less by facts and far more by the hyperboles of tabloid emotion. Such a development should be unsurprising to even the most novice of cultural critics, yet to be in the middle of it, to watch rumor become myth, to see the story stitched out of repetition rather than investigation, was something else entirely. Beck told me, "Right away I saw pack journalism like I have not seen pack journalism in a while. It was really something. I remember going to the courthouse, and somebody would say, 'Hey I understand he got burned'—which wasn't true by the way—'where did he get burned?' And somebody would say, 'Oh, on his face,' and they're all taking notes, and they were sources for each other. They would never say where it came from or who had the information—it was just 'there were burns on his face.'" As Beck watched, the mistakes multiplied. One journalist would announce, "'I did an interview with one of the deputies, and he told me this,' and they would all go with it; no one [else] went and interviewed the deputy. Now part of this is that the deputies and other officials weren't available to us . . . and the same stuff got continually reported." The lead investigator on the case, Sergeant Rob DeBree of the Sheriff's Office, held a press conference early on in an attempt to correct the errors, but, he told me, it didn't seem to make much of a difference—the media had become a closed loop, feeding off their own energies.

As the fall wore on, the distance between Laramie and its broadcast image would become unbridgeable. The court increasingly limited press access to the case and eventually, in the spring, issued a gag order. In response, the Wyoming Press Association wrangled with the court throughout that year over access to hearings and records, suggesting that the court model its treatment of the media on press access guidelines in the Timothy McVeigh trial. Beck assessed Wyoming Public Radio's own performance for me: "I'm not saying we didn't make any mistakes, because we probably did. But I finally got so weary of it I said, 'You know what? If we can't confirm it ourselves, we don't go with it.' It was just too wild."

As the weekend continued, vigils for Matt were held across the nation. By the end of the week, we'd heard word of vigils in Casper, Cheyenne, and Lander (Wyoming towns), Colorado, Idaho, Montana, Iowa, Arizona, Rhode Island, and Pennsylvania. A memorial in Los Angeles attracted an estimated five thousand participants; a "political funeral" in New York City that ended in civil disobedience and hundreds of arrests, about the same. Several hundred mourners lit candles at a vigil outside Poudre Valley Hospital, and a Web site set up by the hospital to give updates about Matt's condition eventually drew over 815,000 hits from around the world.

In Laramie, we held two vigils of our own Sunday night. Jim spoke at the first, held outside the St. Paul's Newman Catholic Center. Father Roger Schmit, the organizer of the event, had contacted him earlier that weekend and asked him to speak. Jim remembers, "I'm sitting here thinking, 'Catholic Church . . . this is not exactly the scene I want to get into.'" But the priest told him, Jim says, "This is such a powerful opportunity—people need to hear from you, and it will help them." Jim thought, "I want to hate him, I want to disagree with him, but I can't." Indeed, such bedfellows would become less strange in the coming months. Matt's death triggered yearlong conversations in several Laramie churches; the Newman Center, the Episcopal church, and the Unitarian-Universalist Fellowship each began discussion groups devoted to questions of sexual orientation and religious doctrine. Father Schmit, the priest Jim regarded with such initial suspicion, would in particular become a vocal advocate for gay tolerance.

I attended that first vigil, which drew nearly one thousand people, a sizable fraction of Laramie's total population. As I crossed Grand Avenue, dodging traffic, the vigil already under way, I was struck by the size and murmurous intensity of the crowd. The speakers included friends of Matt, student leaders, and university officials. Father Schmit had also invited every religious leader in town but found many reluctant to come. The event was genuinely affecting and rightly given over to the desire, as Jim put it, to think of Matt "the person" and not the newly created symbol. While speakers did indeed condemn the homophobia that slid Matt from complicated human being to easy target, others, including Jim, also tried to rehumanize Matt by offering up small details—the nature of his smile, the clothes he liked to wear. The press was there too, of course, and—perhaps inevitably under such circumstances—a faint odor of PR hung in the air. University president Phil Dubois told the assembled, "Nothing could match the sorrow and revulsion we feel for this attack on Matt. It is almost as sad, however, to see individuals and groups around the country react to this event by stereotyping an entire community, if not an entire state."

Stephanie sensed another trouble, a hypocrisy, at work that night:

> There was a tremendous outpouring of support—the vigils, the parade—and a lot of those people—not all of them, not even a substantial portion, but some of those people—if they had known that Matt was gay while he was alive, would have spit on him. But now it was a cause, and that made me upset. Not that I think you can't grieve over this because you're straight or anything like that, but I just questioned the sincerity of some people. And I grew to be very angry at the vigil Sunday night, because it was so like the one I had attended for Steve.

Chapter One

She meant Steve Heyman, a gay man who had been a psychology professor and LGBTA faculty adviser at the university. Heyman was found dead on November 1, 1993, on the edge of Route 70 in Denver. He appeared to have been tossed from a moving car. The case was never solved. To Stephanie, who had known and adored Heyman, the coincidence was unbearable. "It was the same candles, the same fucking hymns. I will never sing 'We are a gentle, angry people' again, because it doesn't change anything. And I'm not going to sing 'We are not afraid today deep in my heart' because I am afraid, and I will always be afraid, and that's what they want, that's why they kill us."

Driven by that anger, Stephanie spoke at the second vigil that night. Much smaller—perhaps one hundred people were in attendance—it was held on the edge of town, at the Unitarian Fellowship. People who went that night tell me it was different from the first. Instead of a lengthy list of official speakers, community members were invited to testify to their mourning, and to their experiences of anti-gay discrimination in Laramie. It was more intense, more ragged, more discomfiting. But both vigils held the same fragile promise of a changed Laramie, a town that—whether it much wanted to or not—would think hard and publicly and not in unison about the gay men and women in its midst, about their safety and comfort and rights.

Later that Sunday night, as the participants in that second vigil left for home, thought about the events of the day, and got ready for bed, Matt Shepard's blood pressure began to drop. He died in the early hours of Monday, October 12th. It was the first day of Gay Awareness Week at the University of Wyoming.

Monday, flags were flown at half-staff on the university campus. Later that week, in Casper, flags were lowered on the day of Matt's funeral to signal a "day of understanding." (According to local newspapers, Wyoming governor Jim Geringer was criticized by the Veterans of Foreign Wars for not following "proper flag etiquette.") That Monday eight hundred people gathered for a memorial service held on Prexy's Pasture, a patch of green in the middle of campus encircled by parking spaces and university buildings and anchored by a statue of "the university family," a happy heterosexual unit of father, mother, and child that one lesbian student, in a letter to the student newspaper, longingly imagined detonating. The memorial service was another exercise in what was becoming a familiar schizophrenia for Laramie residents. Even the layout of the event expressed it: speakers stood in a small clump ringed by sidewalk; spread beyond them was the far larger, shaggy-edged group of listeners. In between the two was an encampment of reporters, flourishing microphones and tape recorders, pivoting cameras back and forth, capturing clips of the speakers and reaction shots of the crowd. It was hard to see past the reporters to the event that had drawn us in the first place, and it was hard to know to a certainty whether we were all there simply to mourn Matt or to make sure that mourning was represented. Not that the second urge was itself necessarily a hypocrisy or a contradiction of the first. It was instead an early manifestation of Laramie's new double consciousness. We didn't simply live here anymore: we were something transmitted, watched, evaluated for symbolic resonance; something available for summary. I suspect a few people naturally sought that televised attention, felt authenticated and confirmed, even thrilled, by the opportunity to be representative; and others seized it, as Walt Boulden had, as a chance to articulate political goals that might otherwise go unheard. Mostly, though, it just pissed people off. As the memorial drew to a close, I walked past satellite vans and the professional autism of TV reporters practicing their opening lines and switching on their solemn expressions and talking to no one in particular.

I was on my way to the first event of Gay Awareness Week. Shortly after the memorial, Leslea Newman, scheduled long before the murder to give the keynote talk, spoke about her gay-themed children's books, which include the oft-censored *Heather Has Two Mommies*. The week's events would be held despite Matt's death, but attendance that evening hadn't necessarily swelled in response—there were maybe seventy folks scattered around in the darkened auditorium. Newman spoke with a bracing, funny, New York brusqueness that scuffed up the audience as she briskly detailed her skirmishes with religious conservatives, and she spoke as well of her sorrow over Matt and her friends' fearful pleading that she cancel her visit to Laramie. They weren't alone in feeling that anxiety; many of the members of the LGBTA were tensed for a backlash as they passed out pro-gay trinkets and "heterosexual questionnaires" at the "Straight But Not Narrow" table in the student union during Awareness Week. They knew the statistics: that anti-gay violence tends to rise sharply in the aftermath of a publicized bashing. But instead, as consoling letters and emails flooded the offices of *The Branding Iron*, the LGBTA, and Wyoming newspapers, supporters flocking to the union tables quickly ran through the association's supplies of buttons and stickers.

As the week dragged on, Laramie residents hung in their windows and cars flyers decrying hate provided by the Wyoming Grassroots Project (a year and a half later, you can still find a few examples around town, stubbornly hanging on). Yellow sashes fluttered from student backpacks; local businesses announced, on signs usually reserved for information about nightly rates, indoor pools, and bargain lunches, their dismay with the crime. The Comfort Inn: "Hate and Violence Are Not Our Way of Life." The University Inn: "Hate Is Not a Laramie Value." Arby's: "Hate and Violence Are Not Wyoming Values 5 Regulars $5.95." Obviously, those signs suggested a typically American arithmetic, promiscuously mixing moral and economic registers. Underneath the sentiment lingered a question: what will his death cost us? But it would be wrong, I think, to see all those gestures as merely cynical calculation, a self-interested weighing of current events against future tourism. We were trying to shape the media summary of Laramie all right, but we were also talking to each other, pained and wondering, through such signs.

Late Monday, about the same time as the Prexy's Pasture memorial, the charges against McKinney, Henderson, and Pasley were upgraded in a closed hearing to reflect Matt's death. Price's charge, the same as Pasley's—accessory after the fact to first-degree murder—was announced at her individual arraignment on Tuesday. In a *20/20* interview that week, Price offered her defense of McKinney and Henderson. She claimed Shepard approached McKinney and Henderson and "said that he was gay and wanted to get with Aaron and Russ." They intended, she said, "to teach a lesson to him not to come on to straight people"—as if torture and murder were reasonable responses to the supposed humiliation of overtures from a gay man. McKinney's father, speaking to the *Denver Post*, argued that no one would care about the crime if his son had killed a heterosexual, which struck me as not exactly on point, even as a media critique. Wyoming's Libertarian gubernatorial candidate (it was an election year) had his own unique twist: he told reporters, "If two gays beat and killed a cowboy, the story would have never been reported by the national media vultures."

Fred Phelps, a defrocked minister, leader of the tiny Kansas Westboro Baptist Church, and author of the Internet site GodHatesFags.com, announced that Monday that he intended to picket Matthew's funeral, scheduled for the coming Friday at St. Mark's Episcopal Church in Casper. His Web site also promised a visit to Laramie on October 19th, but in the end he didn't show. Phelps had made a name for himself in the 1990s as a virulently anti-gay activist, notorious for protesting at the funerals of AIDS victims. Never one to shy from media attention, Phelps faxed reporters images of the signs he and his followers intended to carry at the funeral: "Fag Matt in Hell," "God Hates Fags," "No Tears for Queers." On his Web site, Phelps wrote that "the parents of Matt Shepard did not bring him up in the nature and admonition of the Lord, or he would not have been trolling for perverted sex partners in a cheap Laramie bar." He also, to the bitter laughter of members of the LGBTA, deemed the University of Wyoming "very militantly pro-gay." "The militant homosexual agenda is vigorously pursued" at the university, he proclaimed. At the time of Phelps's statement, the university's equal employment and civil rights regulations did not include sexual orientation as a protected category, nor did the university offer insurance benefits to same-sex partners. President Dubois and the board of trustees, in response to Matt's death, eventually rectified the former failure in September 1999; the latter still remains true to this day. Apparently none of that mattered much in Phelps's estimation, and he would become a familiar figure in Laramie in the months to come.

The Westboro Church's announcement was only one manifestation of the murder's parallel national life, its transmutation into political and religious currency. Matt himself might have been dead, but his image was resurrected by Phelps as well as by his antagonists, and those resurrections, while not invariably hypocritical or grotesque, nevertheless struck me as always risky. Not because we shouldn't talk about Matt, about the murder, looking hard at the facts of it, as well as at its contexts. The risk, it seemed to me, lay in what his image was so often used for in the coming months—the rallying of quick and photogenic outrage, sundered from the hard, slow work for local justice.

On Wednesday, October 14th, the national gay organization the Human Rights Campaign held a candlelight vigil on the steps of the U.S. Capitol, noteworthy if only for the incongruity of an event that paired the likes of Ted Kennedy and Ellen DeGeneres. Jim Osborn was also there—Cathy Renna, a member of GLAAD (Gay and Lesbian Alliance Against Defamation), who had arrived in Laramie the previous weekend to monitor events for her organization, had asked Jim to participate and taken him to Washington. That night, DeGeneres declared that "this is what she was trying to stop" with her television sitcom *Ellen*. The proportions of that statement—the belief that a sitcom could breathe in the same sentence as the brutal vortex of murder—seemed out of kilter to say the least, but it is the age of celebrity politics, after all: Elton John would send flowers to Matt's funeral, Barbara Streisand would phone the Albany County Sheriff's office to demand quick action on the case, and Madonna would call up an assistant to UW president Dubois to complain about what had happened to Matt. Jim Osborn remembers standing next to Dan Butler, an actor on *Frasier*, during the vigil; later, he spotted Kristen Johnston (of *Third Rock from the Sun*) smoking backstage. Attended by numerous federal legislators, the vigil was skipped by Wyoming's two senators, who had announced their sorrow and condemned intolerance in press releases the previous day. The disconnect worked both ways: the Human Rights Campaign, for all its sustained rallying on the national level, never, according to Jim, sent a representative to Laramie until the following summer.

Back in Laramie, on the same day as the D.C. vigil, the university initiated a three-day series of teach-ins on "prejudice, intolerance, and violence" to begin, according to the announcement, "the healing process." The ideas expressed that day were valuable, the sympathies genuine, but I remember feeling overloaded by premature talk of closure. It may have seemed easy for straight mourners to move so quickly, but as Stephanie told me that week, she'd barely begun to realize the extent of her anger. In the face of that, the swiftness of the official move to "healing" seemed at best a well-intended deafness, and indeed, in their outrage by proxy, denunciations of hatred, and exhortations for tolerance, most of the speakers seemed to be talking implicitly and exclusively to straight members of the audience who already agreed.

Many professors on campus also made time in their classes that week to let their students talk about Matt; the university provided a list of teachers willing to facilitate such discussions if individual faculty were uncomfortable raising such an emotionally fraught issue. It was indeed, as Jim Osborn put it, a "teachable moment," and those conversations undoubtedly did real good. One student, who spoke to me on the condition I didn't use his name, told me that before Matt's death he "straight-up hated fags." It hadn't occurred to him that there actually were any gays or lesbians around (a surprisingly common assumption at the university, not to mention in Wyoming generally)—"fag" was a word handy mainly for demeaning other guys in his dorm for "being pussy" (a typical but still depressing conflation of slurs). After seeing students cry in one of his classes as they discussed Matt's death, he had what he called, with a defensive grin, a real breakthrough: he felt a little sick, he told me, that he had thought things about gays that the two killers had probably been thinking about Shepard.

It's impossible to quantify such changes in attitude, but clearly they were happening in many classrooms around campus. Those developments were heartening, but it would be wrong to imply that the changes were immediate or seismic; several students in the coming weeks would describe to me overhearing others saying Matt "got what he deserved." One woman told me that during a class devoted to discussing the murder, "There was a really ugly incident with a couple of guys in the back who were like 'I hate gays and I'm not changing my opinion.'" "People really think that way here," she finished with a resigned expression. In the coming year students and faculty checking out books on gay topics sometimes found them defaced, and in the spring of 1999 vandals defecated on the university's copies of *The Advocate*, a gay magazine.

It would be wrong too to imply that the faculty were perfectly equipped to handle the events of October. When Matt died, there was only one openly gay faculty member on the university campus—Cathy Connelly, a professor of sociology. Since her arrival in 1991, Professor Connelly had periodically taught graduate courses on gay and lesbian issues, but other than Connelly and the small Safe Zone diversity-training group, the university had few resources in place to respond to what had happened. Troubling as well were the reactions of more than one professor I spoke to that week, whose primary responses were to comment on their own uselessness, their own irrelevance—as scholars of obscure fields of inquiry—to such primal issues of life and death. Academics tend to be fairly skilled at self-lacerating narcissism, but it seemed to me at the time an appalling luxury, an indulgence in a kind of intellectual self-pity at a moment when the basic skills of education—critical thinking, articulation, self-reflection—could be so concretely valuable. I wondered about that, and I wondered too when we'd stop talking about how we felt and begin talking about what to do.

Not that public political gestures are always more meaningful than private, emotional ones. On October 15th, the day before Shepard's funeral, the U.S. House of Representatives approved a resolution condemning the murder. Sponsored by Wyoming's sole representative, Barbara Cubin, it struck me as an essentially empty gesture. The nonbinding resolution stated that the House would "do everything in its power" to fight intolerance, and Cubin herself announced that "our country must come together to condemn these types of brutal, nonsensical acts of violence. We cannot lie down, we cannot bury our heads, and we cannot sit on our hands." Stirring stuff, but she also told reporters that day that she opposes federal hate crimes legislation and suggested such things be left up to individual states. So much for "our country coming together." Cubin was not alone, of course, in her contradictory patriotic embrace of Matt; flags were lowered, resolutions passed, in a nation otherwise happy to express its loathing of gays by closeting them in the military, refusing them antidiscrimination protection in most cities and states, repressing their presence in school curricula, faculty, and clubs, and denouncing them in churches. Meanwhile, back in Wyoming that afternoon, a bewildered and frustrated Casper City Council grappled with more concrete resolutions than those that faced the United States Congress. At an emergency meeting to address Phelps's intended picketing of Matt's funeral, the council decided that protesters must stay at least fifty feet from the church. Casper's SWAT team and the Street Drug Unit would be in attendance outside St. Mark's. Streets would be closed nearby the church, the Casper *Star-Tribune* reported, to allow "media satellite vehicles to position themselves."

The funeral on Friday unfurled as a heavy, wet snow fell on Casper. The storm ripped down power lines, cutting electricity in and around Casper; hundreds of cottonwoods and elms lost their branches. Phelps and his handful of protesters (along with another anti-gay protester, W. N. Otwell of Enterprise, Texas) were penned inside black plastic barricades, taunting the huge crowd of mourners, which included strangers, gay and straight alike, drawn to the scene from Cheyenne, Denver, Laramie, and elsewhere. As Charles Levendosky put it a few days later in the *Star-Tribune*, "One thousand others from Wyoming and surrounding states flew or drove into Wyoming to mourn for Matt Shepard, the symbol." While a few mourners engaged in heated debate with the picketers—one carrying a sign reading "Get Back in Your Damn Closet"—most turned their backs to them, the umbrellas pulled out for the snow acting as a fortuitous blockade. To protect the Shepard family from hearing Phelps, the assembled crowd sang "Amazing Grace" to drown out his anti-gay preaching. (The family's loss would intensify that day—Shepard's great uncle suffered what would be a fatal heart attack in the church shortly before the service began.) The funeral inside St. Mark's remained restricted to friends and family of Matt, but a live audio feed carried the service to the First Presbyterian Church nearby. Outside St. Mark's, more mourners ("some wearing black leather," the *Star-Tribune* observed) listened to a KTWO radio broadcast of the service. At the funeral, Matt's cousin Ann Kitch, a minister in Poughkeepsie, New York, delivered the sermon. Emphasizing Matt's gentleness and desire "to help, to nurture, to bring joy to others," she echoed a statement made by Matt's father earlier in the day at a press conference outside city hall: "A person as caring and loving as our son Matt would be overwhelmed by what this incident has done to the hearts and souls of people around the world."

Three days later, the university held yet another memorial service. Around one thousand people heard songs by a multicultural chorus, psalms read by Geneva Perry of the university's Office of Minority Affairs, and statements by Tina Labrie, Jim Osborn, and Trudy McCraken, Laramie's mayor. Rounding out the service was university president Dubois, who made a passionate, personal plea for hate crimes legislation—the political issue that had already, only one week after his death, come to dominate discussions of Matt's murder. "No hate crime statute, even had it existed, would have saved Matt," Dubois read. "But Matt Shepard was not merely robbed, and kidnapped, and murdered. This was a crime of humiliation. This crime was all about being gay. . . . We must find a way to commemorate this awful week in a way that will say to the entire state and nation that we will not forget what happened here."

On Tuesday, October 20th, the Wyoming Lodging and Restaurant Association offered one such response to the nation by passing a resolution in favor of hate crimes legislation. The association was up front about its motivations: to curry favor among tourists who might seek recreation elsewhere. The director was quoted in the Casper *Star-Tribune*: "We want them to know this was an isolated case and could happen anywhere."

⊗

Could happen anywhere indeed. While that oft-repeated phrase was the quick defense offered by many who felt Laramie was being unfairly vilified, it also bumped up against an undeniable truth: in the late 1990s, homosexuality and vehement opposition to it were everywhere in American public culture and politics. Gays in the military, gays in the schools, gays in church, gays in marriage—the place of gay men and lesbians in American culture seemed to be debated in every way possible. For example, on October 14th, two days before Matt's funeral, the Supreme Court upheld a Cincinnati ordinance that denied gays and lesbians legal protection from discrimination in housing, employment, and other public accommodations. Later that autumn Ohio hosted a conference, organized by Focus on the Family, on how to prevent childhood homosexuality; one speaker there, John Paulk, became notorious during the summer of 1998 when he posed with his wife for national newspaper ads announcing that they were former homosexuals "cured" by their faith in God. About the same time the Supreme Court ruled on the city ordinance, the Roman Catholic Archdiocese of Cincinnati announced a deeply contradictory attempt to "reconcile church teachings that denounce homosexual sex as immoral but encourage the loving acceptance of gays." As long as they're celibate, that is—as long as they "live chaste lives." "Hate the sin, love the sinner"—that idea was invoked again and again in Laramie, in church congregations and letters to the editor. But it seems to me that in such visions sexuality slides so intimately close to identity itself that in the end such exhortations call for moral acrobatics requiring an impossible and fundamentally hypocritical kind of dexterity.

Chapter One

Religious justifications were everywhere, of course, in the attacks on homosexuality. Senate Majority Leader Trent Lott, in June 1998, said he learned from the Bible that "you should try to show them a way to deal with [homosexuality] just like alcohol . . . or sex addiction . . . or kleptomaniacs." Pat Robertson announced that "the acceptance of homosexuality is the last step in the decline of Gentile civilization." Bob Jones University in South Carolina instituted a rule banning gay alumni from returning to campus. The religious right boycotted Disney and American Airlines for having policies that refused to discriminate against gays and lesbians. Salt Lake City banned all student clubs rather than allow a gay-straight alliance to continue at one public high school. The Mormon Church donated roughly half a million dollars to supporters of Alaska's Proposition 2, an initiative banning same-sex marriage that succeeded in the fall of 1998. Bans on gay marriage would also pass in Hawaii, California, and West Virginia in the next year and a half. Vermont, with its legalization of gay "civil unions" early in 2000, would be one of the few bright spots.

That Matt's death occurred in the midst of such pervasive anxiety and upheaval might begin to explain why the nation paid attention, but it doesn't stretch very far—his was only one of thirty-three anti-gay murders that year, followed by, in the first months of 1999, a beheading in Virginia and a vicious beating in Georgia. Here in Laramie, we asked a version of that question too: Why Matt, when no one in the media seemed to take a second glance at the other truly awful recent murders we had the grim distinction of claiming? Why Matt, and not Daphne Sulk, a fifteen-year-old pregnant girl stabbed seventeen times and dumped in the snow far from town? Why Matt, and not Kristin Lamb, an eight-year-old Laramie girl who was kidnapped while visiting family elsewhere in Wyoming and then raped, murdered, and thrown in a landfill? Governor Geringer asked those very questions in an October 9th press release, and we asked them too, in Laramie—in letters to the editor, in private conversation. But we didn't always mean the same thing. To some, the media attention to Matt seemed to imply that his death was somehow worse than the deaths of the two girls, and such an implication was genuinely offensive. To some, like Val Pexton, a graduate student in creative writing, it had something to do with the politics of gender: "What happened to [Lamb] was certainly as violent, as hateful, as horrible; and I guess one of my first thoughts was, if [Henderson and McKinney] had done that to a woman, would this have made it into the news outside of Laramie, outside of Wyoming?" And to some, like Jim Osborn, the comparison of Matt to Kristin and Daphne sometimes masked a hostility to gays: "They became incensed—why didn't Kristin Lamb get this kind of coverage, why didn't Daphne Sulk get this kind of coverage? That was the way people could lash out who very much wanted to say, fuck, it was just a gay guy. But they couldn't say it was just a gay guy, so they said, what about these two girls?"

In some ways, it's easy to understand why the media industry seized upon Matt, and why so many responded to the image it broadcast (Judy Shepard, Matt's mother, told *The Advocate* magazine in March 1999 that the family had received "about 10,000 letters and 70,000 emails," as well as gifts, stuffed animals, blankets, and food). Matt was young (and looked younger), small, attractive; he had been murdered in a particularly brutal fashion. The mistaken belief that he had been strung up on the fence provided a rich, obvious source of symbolism: religious leaders, journalists, and everyday people saw in it a haunting image of the Crucifixion, and at the memorial services and vigils for Matt here and elsewhere, that comparison was often drawn. And while Matt had not in reality been put on display in that fashion, the idea that he had been resonated deeply with America's bitter history of ritual, public violence against minorities—many, including *Time* magazine, compared the attack to a lynching. But Matt seemed to provide a source of intense, almost obsessive interest whose explanation lies well beyond these considerations. Perhaps it was merely the insistent repetition of his image in those early days. In the few snapshots that circulated in the press, Matt appeared boyish, pensive, sweet, charmingly vulnerable in oversized wool sweaters—a boy who still wore braces when he died, a boy who looked innocent of sex, a boy who died because he was gay but whose unthreatening image allowed his sexuality to remain an abstraction for many. In my darker moods, I wonder too if Matt invited such sympathy and political outrage precisely because he was dead—if, for many of the straight people who sincerely mourned his murder, he would nevertheless have been at best invisible while alive. To Jim Osborn, the explanation was less dark and more simple: Matt was "someone we can identify with. Matt was the boy next door. He looked like everybody's brother and everybody's neighbor. He looked like he could have been anyone's son."

"He was the nuclear son of the nuclear family." Jay, a Shoshone–Northern Arapahoe–Navajo American Indian born on the Wind River Reservation in the center of Wyoming, is talking to me about the limits of identification. "If that was me hung on the fence, they'd just say, oh, another drunk Indian. No one would have paid much attention." Jay is gay (he uses the Navajo term *nádleeh*—which he translates as "one who loves his own kind"— to describe himself), and while he feels sympathy for Matt, he doesn't feel much kinship. To Jay, the reason why the nation seized upon Matt is just as simple as Jim Osborn's reason but radically different: to Jay, it was as if white, middle-class America finally had its own tragedy. His argument makes some undeniable sense: in a media culture consecrated to repetition, to the endless recopying of the supposed center of American life—white, moneyed, male— Matt did indeed fit the bill, did suit the recycled homogeneities of a still-myopic national culture. For Jay, the tremendous public outpouring of grief, no matter how sincere, remained essentially alienating. When I ask him how people he knows back on the reservation reacted to the murder, he sums up what he describes as a common response, which he himself shared: "Well, at least now one of them"—whites—"knows what we live through every day." Matt learned it, he says. "And one mother now knows, for a little while anyway, what our lives have always been." As he speaks, defiance, resignation, bitterness, and pride mingle in his voice. "Now people might know what our lives are like," what forms of violence—physical, political, cultural—native people experience in the still-hostile territories of the American West.

Jay's home on the reservation was without running water or electricity, but that never felt like deprivation or unusual circumstance to him—"It's just the way it was." When he was nine, Jay moved to Laramie with his family. They arrived after dark. "Laramie looked so beautiful—all these lights spread out—[it] seemed huge to me." He laughs as he describes how he has learned to love the materialism of life off the reservation—"I really, really like having things now," he admits in simultaneous mockery of himself and Anglo consumerism. When I ask him what white residents here don't know about their town, he replies that "Laramie's a nice town"—he likes life here fine—with a pointed caveat: "White people always say there's no bias in Laramie, no racism, but they just don't want to see." Jay has long black hair pulled back in a braid and a round, lived-in face; he's frequently mistaken for Hispanic. As a child, it didn't take him long to stumble across the racial fault lines he describes. In his first year in Laramie, as he walked home from school near the university campus, a college-aged man spit on him. And on the day we talked, a white woman hissed "spic" at Jay minutes before we met. A student at the university, Jay says there is a reason why the October vigils held for Matt were mostly attended by whites: when Matt died and then later, during the legal proceedings against Henderson and McKinney, Jay observes, "you never saw a minority alone on campus—they either left town, or stayed home, or walked in pairs or groups." They were, he and others say, afraid of a backlash—if "someone got killed for being gay, then someone might get killed for being black or Hispanic or native—that's how we felt." In Jay's opinion, the surprise and horror expressed at the vigils—not to mention simply attending them—was almost something of a white luxury: "They felt shock," Jay says, but "I wasn't shocked—I knew this was coming, since I was in high school, seeing the white and Hispanic kids fight. I knew sooner or later someone was going to die." To Jay, risk, the risk of visible difference, didn't seem all that unfamiliar.

Other minority students on campus confirm Jay's point, however melodramatic it might seem to some. Carina Evans, a young woman of Latino and African-American heritage, told me that when the minority community on campus heard that two Latino teenagers had also been attacked by Henderson and McKinney that night, "the immediate response was, oh my God, what about my safety? How safe am I here? And I think our way of dealing with it was just to not talk about it, because I think we figured the less we drew attention to ourselves, the less the chance that something else was going to happen. Which was a sorry response, but a lot of people left town, just did not feel safe, went away for the week or the weekend."* She and others thought, "I'm not going to make myself a target—I'm going to get out of here." No such retaliation was ever reported, but the fact that minority members of the community so feared its possibility that it felt logical to leave town—at the same time that so many white residents could unquestionably consider the attack an isolated incident—reveals something about the complexities of daily life in Laramie.

The divides that run through Jay's and Carina's lives became harder for many in Laramie to ignore in the aftermath of Matt's death. But it was nevertheless a town made defensive by such half-unearthed truths. "Hate is not a Wyoming value," residents kept telling each other, telling visitors, telling the press. "We really take care of each other here," a woman told me one day in a coffee shop, echoing a dearly held ethos I've heard from many in Laramie and that strikes me as generally true. That defensiveness intensified as it encountered the first, clumsy journalistic attempts to offer sociological explanations for the roots of Henderson and McKinney's

---

* A Mexican-American student, Lindsey Gonzales, spoke to me as well about the attack on Morales and Herrera. Lindsey knew Morales quite well (they'd hung out together in the past). She thinks neither the media nor the public cared much about the attack on Morales and Herrera compared to Matt because "they didn't die." But if they had, she speculates, people probably wouldn't have cared much more. When I ask her why, she says she's not sure, but she speculates that racial prejudice is simply more "familiar," something with a longer and better-known history in America, whereas "we're all just getting used to" homosexuality right now, and "that made it a big deal."

violence, attempts that implied—to us here, anyway—that Laramie was to blame. Perhaps the most locally reviled version was an article written by Todd Lewan and Steven K. Paulson for the Associated Press that appeared in October, an occasionally persuasive attempt at class analysis hamstrung by bad facts and a love affair with the thuddingly clichéd symbolic density of the railroad tracks that cut through town. Here is their Laramie:

> On the east side is the University of Wyoming's ivy-clad main campus, where students drive sports cars or stroll and bike along oak-shaded sidewalks. On the opposite side of town, a bridge spans railroad tracks to another reality, of treeless trailer parks baking in the heavy sun, fenced-off half-acre lots, stray dogs picking for scraps among broken stoves, refrigerators, and junked pickups. Unlike the university students, youths on the west side have little in the way of entertainment: no malls, no organized dance troupes, no theater or playing fields.

Blowing holes in this picture is still a local sport, more than a year after the murder. Bob Beck, for example, takes fairly comprehensive aim at the story:

> They decided that the reason a murder like this happened was because those of us, including me, who live in west Laramie, the "other side of the tracks," are underprivileged, don't have benefits, all this stuff. Because we're over there, we're obviously looking to get even with the good side of the tracks and are going to commit a crime like this. [They] basically blamed the fact that some of us who live in west Laramie don't have a mall (meanwhile there isn't a mall on the east side either); so we don't have a mall, we don't have paved streets, apparently don't have trees. And this is the reason for all this violence? That was one of the most damaging stories in retrospect, because it got picked up by just about every major paper. A lot of people got their impressions of the case from that.

The list of mistakes could continue: Henderson and McKinney didn't even live in west Laramie; oaks rarely grow at seven thousand feet; and few university students drive fancy sports cars—

more likely, like many of the students I've encountered, they're working fifteen to thirty hours a week to pay their tuition, maybe at the same Taco Bell where Henderson worked as a teenager. It's hard to choose, but my personal favorite is the anguished hand-wringing over west Laramie's lack of organized dance troupes. Organized dance troupes?

Plenty of folks I've spoken to volunteer that they live on the west side and are quick to say they're "not trash," that they like the rustic character of west Laramie's unpaved streets, that they don't necessarily feel excluded from "Laramie proper," despite, for example, the west side's usual lack of representation on the city council. And I've found few residents who weren't offended by such shallow press characterizations of Laramie, who didn't argue that status doesn't matter much here, that Laramie is friendly and easygoing and safe, that most folks don't even bother to lock their doors. All their points of rebuttal are well taken, and indeed they're reasons why many love to live here. But nevertheless I think the eager rapidity with which so many of us rejected such examples of journalistic ineptitude masked at times a certain unease—and sometimes a hardworking amnesia—about the subtle realities of class, sexuality, and race here in Laramie. Those realities may be too complicated to sum up through the convenient shorthand of railroad tracks and trailer parks, but they still flow, hushed yet turbulent, beneath daily life in this town.

CHAPTER TWO

A town is not a culture, not precisely. Drive ten blocks in any direction in Laramie, and perhaps the most you could say that is definitively shared by the lives you move past is that they happen under the same quixotic weather, surrounded by the same light-struck, wind-cut plain. Cultures—in the sense of shared beliefs, attitudes, stories, identities—only come clear at levels much smaller or much larger than towns, in the furtive subcultures beloved by cultural anthropologists or, alternately, in the nation imagined, inflated, and set afloat by media conglomerates. A town is not a culture, especially a town marked by the ebb-and-flow vagrancies of college life, a town in a state with a stalled economy and a net population loss every year.

That's not to say that nothing can be said of Laramie; instead it's simply to say that to call Laramie "hateful" makes little sense, because it seems to presume some kind of handshake has happened among its residents, to presume that a place can fall into a clean grid of explanation, without blur or contradiction. Laramie is rife with mundane contradictions: a town populated by Cowboy Saloons, Chuckwagon Cafés, and Rancher Restaurants in a county whose primary employer is the university, in a state where ranching accounts for only 3 percent of the economy and landscaping is the fastest-growing profession in the agricultural sector; a relatively liberal town in the self-dubbed "Equality State," which granted women the right to vote while still a territory in 1868 and shortly thereafter barred them from serving on juries for the next eighty years. But if a town is not quite a culture, still it seems crucially important to see whether something about Laramie can explain, if not what happened to Matt, at least what is here to make such a thing possible.

The low-angle shots of the fence that appeared in most magazines and newspapers that fall made it look as if Matt, and the town itself, were abandoned hard on the edge of nowhere. And the high prairie can feel that way. It's a landscape whose vast scope and extremity make everything on it seem fugitive: the uprooted sagebrush skittering across it, the antelope herds fading into its bleached tones, the prefab ranch houses laid low against the obstreperous wind. It's also a landscape whose emptiness can threaten to make anything set against it iconic—no fence, it seems, could lend itself to such instantly grand and singular symbolism as that buck fence on the prairie that Henderson and McKinney, not especially high-order symbolic thinkers themselves, nevertheless chose as the stage for their own remorselessness.

But cock the camera at a different angle, and you'd see something altogether different: Sherman Hills, one of the more upscale housing developments in Laramie, within a half mile of the spot where Matt was tied (and where McKinney resided for a while as a child). Close to the east, the prairie furrows and bumps into the Laramie range, the whole stretch an accessible and much-used landscape for trail running and mountain biking. The hum of Interstate 80 is just audible to the south. A new Super Wal-Mart is going up near the turnoff Henderson and McKinney took to the fence. The Mountain Cement plant pumps a steady vertical plume of white vapor to the west, and thirty miles beyond it lies the Snowy Range, a long, rugged spur of the Rockies that rises to twelve thousand feet and draws a thin but steady stream of hikers in summer and snowmobilers and skiers in winter. Custom ranchette subdivisions on the outskirts of town lap the edges of cattle ranches. The horror of Matt's death to me always seemed not that he lay in stark isolation but that he lay alone so close to so many and so much.

That's not to imply that Laramie isn't also marked by a kind of lonesomeness. The fifty miles of interstate that lie between Laramie and Cheyenne, Wyoming's capital, probably qualify as one of the state's more populous corridors, but for someone accustomed to the gas stations, strip malls, and fast-food restaurants that encrust most highways it sure doesn't look it: except for a single roadside cafe, the Vedauwoo parking lot ("no services"), and the Lincoln memorial rest area ("the highest point on Route 80"), there's simply no place to stop, and the only significant lights you see at night are the long, ghostly rows of truckers' rigs parked alongside the highway for a few hours' rest. From Laramie, Route 80 takes you either east to Cheyenne or west to Rawlins; Fort Collins, Colorado, is sixty miles to the south, Casper a few hours north. The roads to each close periodically in the winter (which here can last well into May) because of treacherous weather—high winds, black ice, blowing snow that snakes across the blacktop or surrounds you in a whiteout, making for zero visibility ahead and behind even with clear sky above. It's true there's not much else between Laramie and those other places, if by "much else" you mean large populations and consumer opportunities. If you mean something different, then you might understand the draw to live here.

Of course, plenty of people in Laramie don't particularly feel that draw; one icebreaker sure to work at faculty gatherings is to mention the lack of cheese selection in town, or maybe the dearth of sushi. But it doesn't take too many conversations to learn what you might get instead—space, quiet, calm, and austere, spreading beauty.

☙

Before a town sprang up here to greet the Union Pacific railroad in 1868, these high plains were familiar only to Indian tribes such as the Sioux, Shoshone, and Arapahoe and, by the early 1800s, to trappers like Jacques LaRamie, a French Canadian, and Jim Beckwourth, the first African American recorded in the Wyoming territories. Laramie was named for the river where LaRamie had died fifty years before, apparently at the hands of Indians; in 1868, the year the town was founded, it was mostly railroad tracks, saloons, and whorehouses. Cattle came quick, but any thought that they'd be easy money died a brutal death in the winter of 1886–87, when the blizzards never seemed to let up and cattle died across the West by the hundred thousand, buried in towering drifts and carcass-clogged ravines. No matter the cowboy myth, Wyoming was by then already seeking other sources of profit, signing and breaking land treaties with the tribes as it went. The ranching life, tough and sinewy, remained to shoulder up the state's own sense of itself, but the real cash was to be found elsewhere, in Wyoming's almost unimaginably rich mineral resources—coal and later, oil, trona, uranium, and natural gas.

Cattle and minerals: the up-and-down fortunes of beef, coal, and oil would fuel Wyoming's boom-and-bust economy straight through the twentieth century and into the twenty-first. By the 1990s the mineral industries had vast financial capital, ranchers had powerful symbolic capital, if far less economic strength, and both had serious political clout in the state legislature. But if Wyoming today is mineral-rich, it is also remarkably cash-poor, a resource colony for national and international corporate interests that lie far outside its borders. According to the Equality State Policy Center, a watchdog coalition of environmentalist, labor, and progressive organizations that monitors the state's economy and budget, Wyoming is right to feel like a colony (and indeed that is a description that many state residents often bitterly employ).* In their fall 1999 publication, as a budget crisis loomed in the state legislature, the policy center suggested that Wyoming had kowtowed to the mineral industries, timidly holding down taxes on extracted resources that could actually be considered the property of state residents (most of Wyoming's coal, trona, oil, and gas production happens on public lands, not lands privately owned by industry). Tom Throop, the center's amiable director, mostly blames that reluctance on the powerful influence of the minerals lobby on the state legislature (during the 2000 budget session, Throop told me, the Cheyenne airport was clogged with corporate jets ferrying lobbyists into Wyoming.)

Those lobbyists argue in return that the mineral industries pay a heavy tax burden to the state and also provide Wyoming with much-needed jobs. It's certainly true that Wyoming, with only a tiny manufacturing sector and even less high-tech employment, can use jobs: but according to Throop, work in the mineral industries has declined even as production has skyrocketed. The policy center argues that from 1987 to 1997 coal production rose 110 percent in the state (Wyoming's Powder River Basin coal is remarkably clean-burning, a valuable commodity in the post–Clean Air Act United States); at the same time, employment in the coal industry actually decreased 1 percent, while coal producers enjoyed the expiration of certain state taxes. Anyway you crunch those numbers, Wyoming seems to be losing.

Taxes on minerals, along with sales and property taxes, do indeed prop up the state's budget. Wyoming has no state income tax—a fiercely guarded fact of life here—so state and local governments must seek revenue elsewhere. Such revenue decisions often seem to reconfirm Wyoming's sense that it is a colony beholden to outside interests: food and clothing—items mostly purchased by locals—are typically subject to sales taxes, while tourist amenities like float trips and lift tickets regularly escape unscathed. Teton

---

* My favorite, if somewhat more frivolous, example of Wyoming's colonial status was the possibility in 1999 that an offshore medical school, located in the U.S. Virgin Islands, would open a branch campus in Casper.

County, a vacation hot spot and favored location for absentee gentleman ranchers, has the nation's highest average annual income, around $88,000 (Albany County's average income, by comparison, is roughly $60,000 less); meanwhile, service workers in Teton County's famed Jackson Hole live in tents during the summer or find themselves squeezed out of the state altogether and forced to commute from cheaper towns in Idaho.

Overall, the economic picture for Wyoming is fairly stark. Wyoming's considerable draws—its low population (480,000 people), its gorgeous, empty spaces, and lack of urban and suburban sprawl—are also paradoxically what keep manufacturing and high-tech investment at bay. The giddy growth of the nation's economy in the 1990s lagged in Wyoming. Members of the arriviste dot.com set might vacation here but have rarely chosen Wyoming as a home for new businesses. The 2000 legislature's budget crisis was offset by rising oil prices and—this strikes me as almost funny—an unexpected windfall in inheritance taxes. But such revenue sources are unpredictable, to say the least, and while Laramie, unlike the rest of the state, might have its university and its close proximity to Colorado populations, it shares Wyoming's difficult economic fortunes.

Laramie today might seem affluent enough to an outsider passing through (as it did to the author of a 1999 *Nation* article who, gushing about flaky pastries and pretty jewelry, bizarrely compared the town to Brooklyn's Park Slope). Downtown, you can indeed get your fill of Patagonia, cappucino, and expensive pottery. The "tree area"—a name my neighbors and I usually say with a self-mocking grin—is a cottonwood-lined neighborhood due east of downtown and home to some beautiful old bungalows. On the edges of town, fat, expensive trophy homes are multiplying. But look closer, and the picture is less simple. Sit with your latte enough weeks in a row, and you'll probably see a new business fail downtown. The business parks and specialty superstores that crowd the edges of so many American towns have yet to arrive. Pawnshops and cash-checking loan joints with cheerily inappropriate names like Mr. Money and Mo' Money outnumber the pottery outlets by a wide margin. And not everyone is living in a restored bungalow or custom-built house, not by a long shot.

Lyn Lyles, director of the Interfaith/Good Samaritan agency in the winter of 1999–2000, is a fast-talking, blunt, and angry advocate for the poor of Laramie. Laramie, she tells me, has some truly terrible substandard housing—uninsulated trailers with ancient, malfunctioning appliances; homes with no heat, no electricity, no running water (Aaron McKinney himself lived for a while in a converted stable that lacked a stove and refrigerator; Henderson resided among a thin trickle of battered trailers down by the cement plant). During her tenure Lyn handled a case in which a father had to rescue his daughter from her bedroom in the middle of the night: the ceiling was raining down in chunks on top of her.

Interfaith is a nondenominational organization that scrapes together public and private funds and collaborates with other agencies to provide much-needed emergency assistance to the poor. In 1999 Interfaith served around 13 percent of Albany County's population, distributing $97,000 to four thousand men, women, and children (15 percent of the county's residents officially lived below the poverty line in 1995). As in many other states, antipoverty groups such as Interfaith serve a crucial if underfunded role in the postwelfare America of dwindling cash assistance and government agencies that Lyn calls "lethargic" (but "not hostile") in their mission to aid the poor. As Interfaith's director, Lyn sees a side of Laramie that many miss: "This community thinks they're the most accepting, nondiscriminatory community in Wyoming. But there are two communities here. There is the Laramie community, and there is the university community." By the "university community" Lyn means the faculty and administration—not the students or the lower-paid staff. "The university community are good people, but they don't know what's going on."

What's going on, for example, is a peculiarly rural kind of homelessness. Not many people see it, according to Lyn, because it doesn't take its most familiar form here: the homeless in Laramie mostly don't live on the street. It's too cold for that, although the truly desperate have in the past huddled beneath the Clark Street viaduct that connects east and west Laramie. Instead, they live, Lyn says, in cars, in tents, or in unbearably overcrowded conditions. One client of Lyn's was a single mother living by fragile invitation with sixteen other people in a three-bedroom trailer. While she might have a roof over her head, the profound uncertainty, the impossible lack of private space, the financial straits that put her there in the first place and prevent her from getting out—those are indeed the conditions of homelessness.

Those financial straits aren't uncommon in a state where nearly 30 percent of schoolchildren qualify for free or reduced-price lunches and where, as the 1990s drew to a close, real wages ranked among the four or five lowest in the nation. Unemployment dropped a bit here in the late 1990s, but at least one economist, Richard O'Gara at the Center for Economic and Business Data in Cheyenne, reckoned that the drop was due not so much to an increase in good jobs as to an out-migration of people leaving the state to seek employment elsewhere. And according to Lyn and O'Gara, the problem isn't so much unemployment, it's underemployment. Pay is so low in most work that one job won't keep your head above water; Wyoming workers can look forward to making seventy-seven cents for every dollar earned by the average United States worker. Some employers advertise full-time work, Lyn observes, but then actually hire new workers at twenty hours per week to avoid paying for benefits and workers' compensation. The result is that Wyoming is a state where 10 percent of workers juggle three or more jobs at a time. As in Laramie, those jobs are often poorly benefited agricultural labor work or service jobs cleaning motels and houses, clerking in stores, or dishing up food. They tend to pay wages hovering well under ten dollars an hour. Construction work might pay a bit better, but the employment tends to be seasonal and uncertain. (McKinney and Henderson were both roofers, a job with a short season that provided, according to Henderson's request for court-appointed counsel, $900 a month in take-home pay, out of which Russell ponied up $350 in monthly rent.) There honestly isn't much else, unless you're lucky enough to land a job at the university, or the cement plant, or Ivinson Memorial Hospital. Take Mary Jane Trout (a pseudonym), for example: when Mary Jane, an experienced schoolteacher with an education degree, first moved to town, the only work she could find was handing out food samples at a local grocery store.

To Lyn, these experiences of economic drudgery and frequent humiliation help to explain Wyoming's high rates of domestic violence and drug abuse. In 1997 Wyoming ranked eighth nationally in domestic violence murders; that same year, Wyoming teenagers were twice as likely as teens nationwide to have used methamphetamine, a cheap, intense high that's easy to cook up at home and has become the drug of choice in the Rocky Mountain West (according to JoAnn Wypijewski's reporting in *Harper's*, Henderson and McKinney were themselves frequent tweakers). At Interfaith, Lyn sees with mounting frustration what she considers to be the class barriers thrown up in Laramie by these cruel conditions. Unlike the many who attacked the notorious Associated Press article, she thinks these exclusions did indeed have something to do with Matt's murder: "The barrier was put up a long time ago to these kids [McKinney and Henderson]. They were left out and never invited in. If you keep seeing everything you can't have and can't do and can't be, you'll prey on the weaker."

While Interfaith serves mostly white residents of Laramie (which makes statistical sense—over 90 percent of Laramie is white), it has been trying to reach out to Hispanic residents, Laramie's largest minority community at 7 percent, by hiring bilingual volunteers. Lyn herself, she tells me, is half-Hispanic, but, blonde-haired and blue-eyed, she's rarely taken to be. She is careful to note that she knows of no official studies of racial discrimination in Albany County, but anecdotally, in her interactions with clients, she has come to feel a certain prejudice exists against the Hispanic community in Laramie—a prejudice not expressed in the kind of violence Matt fell prey to but more commonly through small humiliations and informal segregations.

꩜

Lindsey Gonzales, a young woman of Mexican and Anglo heritage who grew up in Laramie and now attends the university, feels those burdens, not as absolute barriers but instead as subtle yet frustrating accompaniments to her daily life in Laramie. Echoing Jay, Lindsey feels too that white residents are uncomfortable with the thought that bias might exist in their town: "They want to think there's nothing like that in Laramie. They don't want to see racist people or prejudiced people—they don't want to say our community has people like that. They say, oh no, Laramie's a perfect place to bring up your kids. . . . Well . . . ," she laughs good-naturedly, "it's not. At the elementary school I went to"—on the east side of town—

> there was me and one other guy that was Hispanic. I was embarrassed at my last name, because no one else had that last name. My grandma bought me a brand-new backpack, and she put my name on it in masking tape, and before I got to school I ripped off my last name because I felt like it wasn't the norm—it wasn't Smith or Jones. And I felt like people would make fun of me because I had a different last name from everybody else. So I grew up that way and I didn't really start hanging out with people of my own race until high school. I don't know why it was that I didn't, but I never did until high school. Now I feel more comfortable in that group than I do with people of other backgrounds, because I feel like I can relate to them.

Despite her childhood anxieties, Lindsey has had few direct experiences of verbal harassment, perhaps because she's not "obviously" Hispanic in appearance. Dark-haired but light-skinned, she says, "I may not look it, but I am." When a high school classmate discovered her background, she said to Lindsey, "All right—then show me your gun." That's at worst a trivial form of ignorance, and Lindsey today is straightforward and fiery enough that she doesn't care to let such stuff slide. And, Lindsey points out, she found Laramie High School's atmosphere quite supportive. Lindsey was a member of a multicultural group chosen to increase awareness at the school about racial and ethnic issues. She speaks fondly of experiences with the group, and she now seeks out courses in the university's new Chicano/a studies program. (Lindsey's grandmother didn't speak English when she began elementary school; two generations later, Lindsey has begun to study Spanish.)

Lindsey is quick to assert that the Hispanic community is not at all homogeneous and certainly not (counter to common stereotypes) entirely poverty-stricken. They run the gamut from rich to poor; Lindsey herself falls somewhere in the middle. Her father manages Safeway's dairy section, her mother works as a legal secretary for the county attorney's office, and Lindsey works part-time to help cover the costs of her schooling. Lindsey is a third-generation Laramie resident—her paternal grandmother came to Laramie from Las Truchas, New Mexico, her paternal grandfather from Mexico. Her family's employment history includes the railroad and sheep herding—Wyoming work for certain. Despite that, Lindsey feels Hispanics are often funneled into certain jobs in Laramie. "You can see it at this university," she says, where Hispanic workers fill many custodial positions but are radically underrepresented in faculty and administration jobs.

Laramie's Hispanic community endured fairly intense residential segregation for much of the twentieth century, herded into a narrow strip hard on the western side of the railroad tracks (the rest of "west Laramie" lies more than a mile beyond, separated from the old Hispanic neighborhood by the Little Laramie River and Route 80). Much of the Hispanic community still resides on those streets (often by choice, Lindsey notes), but she points out that speaking of a "Hispanic community" lures one into complicated territory. It's a community insofar as it shares a residential history, but Lindsey says it would be an exaggeration to say all Laramie Hispanics "celebrate their heritage" in the same fashion or feel a strong communal pull. The Latin American Club, a social organization whose building lies on the southern outskirts of town, was active in the past—Lindsey remembers going to dances there as a child—but today, she says, she knows of little happening there.

But if Hispanic residents like Lindsey don't experience the deeply entrenched structural racism of Wyoming's (and America's) past, certain subtleties of isolation and surveillance still permeate their daily experience. Laramie whites—especially upper-class whites—and Hispanics "only come together when they want to eat Mexican," Lindsey says with a rueful laugh (not that our local restaurants "represent Mexican food very well," she adds). If not legally segregated, Laramie still feels socially split to her along ethnic lines. And that social division sometimes has its consequences: "Me and my best friend"—who is African American—"have this joke every time we go into Kmart," Lindsey says. When they hear a "security scan" announcement over the loudspeaker, they laugh and respond, "We're leaving, we're leaving!" But they joke about that kind of racial suspicion, Lindsey says, "because it is there. People watch you like a hawk."

Carina Evans tells me something similar: "There's a low-level anxiety" to being a minority in Laramie, she observes, and "maybe a false sense of security: as long as I don't think about it, I just go to class or to work and go home, I'm going to be okay. If I'm not out there stirring anybody up, I'm going to be okay." She doesn't buy the argument she has heard often that white Wyoming residents, by virtue of the state's relative homogeneity, simply don't have the chance to grow comfortable with minorities: "There's a false sense of 'I have a blank slate, I'm from a small town, I've never been in contact with these kinds of things.' When in reality they probably have, but they've just chosen to not associate with people like that. I think it's kind of an excuse." Val Pexton, a white woman who grew up on a cattle ranch outside Douglas, Wyoming, agrees that Wyoming folks often feel a certain discomfort in the presence of most kinds of visible difference: "We'll say we don't get into anybody's else's business. . . . They say that on the one hand but on the other hand they really are on the lookout for anybody who is different. If that person keeps it real low key . . . then they're okay, they're left alone. But the minute they move out of that safe zone, then the tolerance is gone."

Carina was born and raised in Cheyenne. The air force base located on the city's edge is racially diverse, but according to

Carina, "they stay on the base mostly—they don't come into the Cheyenne community." Carina describes her minority childhood in Cheyenne: "It's an edgy feeling there, because the town is segregated along racial lines. The south side"—where Carina lived— "is predominantly Hispanic, and there's no city planning or city development that goes on there in general; and when there is, people wonder, 'Why are you wasting money on the south side, when you could be building a soccer park or something up north?'" In elementary school and junior high, Carina's classmates were mostly Hispanic and black. Later, in high school, the racial makeup shifted radically; her high school classes (at Cheyenne's Central High) were predominantly white. "There were a lot of problems in school then, a lot of tension." But it was rarely addressed: "I don't really remember anybody talking about race; I don't think I really even became conscious that I was a minority until I came to college. I think I tried so hard to pretend that I wasn't, that I could fit in."

In a Casper *Star-Tribune* article published the day before Matt died, a UW student, who as a teenager had moved to Cheyenne from Hong Kong, summed up the point of view that I have heard most frequently in my interviews with minority residents: "Just because they don't call you names and they don't beat you up doesn't mean they really accept you." And perhaps that's the form much bigotry takes, not merely in Wyoming but in post–civil rights America generally—a fogged and treacherous region where the most violent and legalized discriminations of the past have begun to fade but the beliefs that generated them still linger, mutating, feinting, harder to see, for both those still struggling in the grip of such attitudes and those who feel their lives fenced in by them.

To advocates of bias crimes legislation, that poor visibility seems to have settled in for the long haul in Cheyenne, the seat of Wyoming's state government, where the weather has been hostile to their cause since the early 1990s.* During that stretch, bias crimes law has become the primary focus of debates about discrimination in Wyoming. Senator Mike Massie, a Democratic legislator from Laramie, offered me a crash course in that history one unseasonably warm March morning, in his small, unprepossessing house on the north side of town. (Such a casual meeting is actually quite typical of politics Wyoming-style—citizens feel pretty free to call up the governor and state legislators and speak their mind, a sensible presumption in a state where over 70 percent of the population regularly votes in general elections.) Only a few weeks earlier, during the state senate's 2000 session, Massie had sponsored a bias crimes bill. It didn't get very far: the introduction of the bill for debate was defeated eighteen to twelve. But Massie tells me he intends to keep at it, cautiously optimistic that bias crimes legislation will eventually pass in Wyoming. Massie is a tall man with an open face and a calming style; while we talk, his ancient tabby cat wanders by periodically to invite a scratch. Democrats like Massie are a small minority in the legislature— Wyoming, a state with a wide libertarian streak, has a long history of conservative politics. (It is not, however, the haven for militia members and antigovernment tax protesters people outside the state seem to fantasize it must be. For example, when a white supremacist in Casper ran for office in the late 1980s, he was solidly opposed by a grassroots effort that quickly mobilized against him. And in the winter of 2000, when a reporter from Gillette called me to see if I knew of any extreme-right organizations operating in the state, he admitted he'd had difficulty unearthing any himself.)

Massie tells me that the first attempt to introduce a bias crimes bill in the state legislature took place in 1994 (bills addressing "malicious harassment" had failed earlier in the decade, in 1990

---

* The terms "bias crime" and "hate crime" seem to be used interchangeably, at least in most lay discussions of this kind of legislation. I use the term "bias crime" throughout this chapter because it reflects the language of the laws considered in Wyoming and because it seems to me to describe the intended target of that legislation more precisely.

and 1991). The 1994 bill and its future versions were the result of solid grassroots lobbying by, among other organizations, the NAACP, the United Gays and Lesbians of Wyoming, the Wyoming Grassroots Project, and the Wyoming Church Coalition, a diverse group of state religious leaders; and each version has had bipartisan sponsorship in the legislature. The 1994 bill, sponsored by Republican representative Harry Tipton of Lander—a stalwart supporter of bias crimes legislation throughout the 1990s—proposed making bias crimes a new category of crime. Massie tells me that choice "ran into a lot of constitutional questions, especially from the ACLU, who wondered if that trampled too far over into freedom of speech and action. The bill never made it out of committee."

As a result, when bias crimes legislation returned to the agenda the following year, its supporters suggested a different approach, patterned after a Wisconsin state law that had been unanimously upheld by the United States Supreme Court in 1993. The new bill called for increased penalties for crimes committed if the victimized person was intentionally selected (in the stiffly ineloquent language of the law) "in whole or in part because of the actor's belief or perception regarding the race, religion, color, disability, sexual orientation, national origin, or ancestry of that person or the owner or occupant of that property, whether or not the actor's belief or perception was correct." (The part about perception, which might seem odd, is actually quite important; according to the National Gay and Lesbian Task Force, attacks on heterosexuals perceived as gay rose 36 percent in 1996.) The challenge to the Wisconsin law resulted from a case in which several black men had been charged with bias crimes for attacking a white man; thus, Massie told me, "those who later on in Wyoming claimed that [the proposed legislation] was setting up a special status for certain groups of people didn't understand the history of the early law that the Wyoming attempts were based upon." Like much civil rights and antidiscrimination law before it, the language of the bias crimes proposal did not single out certain groups (blacks, for example, or gays); it instead identified categories of identity, status, and belief that had operated historically as tense fault lines in American culture. The 1995 bill, which was cosponsored by Massie, generated much less opposition from the ACLU and civil libertarians who were concerned about freedom of speech: "What the '95 law did and what subsequent efforts have done is to enhance an existing crime; bias itself can never be a crime, it can only be used to enhance" the penalty for an already established crime.

What did generate opposition, according to both Massie and activists I've spoken to, was the inclusion of sexual orientation as a category. Sexuality has not been the only point of controversy—some legislators, according to Massie, have simply considered already existing criminal penalties adequate to the job—but it has been nevertheless a powerful impediment to passage. Joe, a member of the United Gays and Lesbians of Wyoming, told me shortly after Matt's death that he and other supporters of the legislation had been led to understand that if sexual orientation were dropped from the bill it would have a chance at passing. In a show of solidarity, other organizations, including the Wyoming Church Coalition, refused to compromise; in 1995 the bill again failed.

"The bill has had an interesting life since then," Massie tells me, if monotonous in result: the inclusion of sexual orientation has continued to generate opposition, and every version of the bill since 1995 has failed—but not always in the same way. After a hiatus in 1996—a budget session, during which it is statutorily difficult to introduce nonbudget items into the agenda—bias crimes legislation returned in 1997 and made some brief headway. That year, the bill (identical in language to the 1995 version) was passed seven to two by the house Judiciary Committee but then died "on general file": it was never introduced to the entire floor for debate. Debate on an identical "mirror" bill in the senate was indefinitely postponed by the senate Judiciary Committee. That same session witnessed a bill opposing gay marriages die a similar and possibly related death. Calling for legalized "invalidity of same-sex marriages," that bill reflected a nationwide trend in which numerous state legislatures rushed to outlaw gay marriages, to combat what at the time was the entirely hypothetical possibility that another state might legalize same-sex marriage, thus forcing other states under federal law to recognize such relationships. The bill passed the house Labor, Health, and Social Services Committee by a six-to-three vote, but then it too died on general file. Pat Nagel, a Republican representative from Casper who supports bias crimes legislation, told me that the failure of the two bills was unrelated, but many gay and lesbian residents of the state with whom I've spoken feel differently, finding it hard to believe that two bills enswirled by the controversy over gay rights wouldn't meet an interlinked fate. Mike Massie couldn't confirm those suspicions but thought it possible that both bills languished on general file in what might have been a spur-of-the-moment trade-off: by introducing neither bill, the house could forestall what would be an ugly debate about homosexuality, deep-six the bias crimes legislation, and tell its supporters that while their bias crimes bill had failed, so, at least, had the bill opposing gay marriage—and they could assuage the proponents of the marriage bill with the opposite line. Whether linked or not, the fate of the two bills satisfied neither those who desired more legal protections for gays and lesbians nor those who did not.

Certainly that outcome did not satisfy those calling for bias crimes law, who continued their pressure and were slowly building wider support in the legislature. In the winter of 1998, another budget session, the bill was sponsored once again in the senate, and, as in 1996, it did not receive the two-thirds vote necessary to introduce a nonbudget bill (the vote that year was sixteen to twelve against, with two excused). When the bias crimes debate returned in 1999, the terrain had shifted radically. Matt Shepard was dead, the Human Rights Campaign and other major gay and lesbian organizations had made him the central symbol in their fight for bias crimes laws throughout America, and the nation was looking on to see how Wyoming would respond.

The state legislature that winter would consider, with varying degrees of intensity, seven bills addressing bias crimes. One merely asked for the gathering and study of bias crimes data; the other six, in different manners, sought stiffened penalties for crimes motivated by bias. Wende Barker, a Laramie resident, former state legislator, and leader of the Wyoming Bias Crimes Coalition, and John Little, the president of UGLW that winter, were among those lobbying hard for the bills; I and many others received frequent updates from Barker through an email list she faithfully ran during the legislative session. Senate File 84, sponsored by Jayne Mockler, a Democrat from Cheyenne, and its mirror version in the house, Bill 132, sponsored by Tipton, Nagel, and others, were seen by activists like Barker and Little as the strongest bills and ones with the best bet for passage, modeled as they were directly on the Wisconsin measure. The two initiatives differed from the four other "enhanced penalty" proposals in several critical ways. First, unlike two of their competitors (HB 206 and SF 091), the favored bills included the "laundry list" of named categories—race, religion, color, disability, sexual orientation, national origin, and ancestry—that had already withstood judicial scrutiny and had appeared in the 1995, 1997, and 1998 Wyoming legislative proposals. The competition—HB 206 and SF 091—merely directed enhanced penalties against crimes motivated by "prejudice against a group"—profoundly vague language that most likely would fail a court challenge.

Second, SF 84 and HB 132 were broadest in scope: they allowed enhancement of penalties for both misdemeanor crimes and felonies. House Bills 117 and 206 did so only for misdemeanors, and HB 215 limited its discussion to first-degree murder (it also addressed itself only to murders "motivated by hate of the victim's race, religion, or personal lifestyle," a list some supporters of bias crimes legislation deemed incomplete and vulnerable to judicial challenge). Finally, the two bills favored by the Bias Crimes Coalition tried to assuage two pressing concerns of its opponents, who argued that such legislation might put a defendant's entire past on trial and would grant special status to certain groups. Both SF 84 and HB 132 required that evidence of biased "expressions and associations" could only be introduced at trial if such expression or association "relates to the crime charged and is reasonably contemporaneous to the underlying offense." In other words, prosecutors, seeking evidence of prejudice, would not be given free rein to dredge up a defendant's distant past. And for those who argued that bias crimes law would establish "special rights," the bills maintained that nothing in the proposed statute would "confer" or "expand" any "civil rights or protections to any group or class identified under this section beyond those rights or protections that exist under the federal or state constitution or the civil laws of the state of Wyoming."

As the session wore on, legislators and activists in support of enhanced penalties increasingly focused their energies on the two mirror bills. House Bills 117, 206, and 215 were withdrawn by their sponsors, and the house Judiciary Committee, after deleting the felony provisions, approved HB 132 for debate on the house floor. Meanwhile, the senate Judiciary Committee stalled discussion of Files 84 and 91 while it waited to see the results of the house vote. The house bill passed first and second reading by the slimmest of margins, but the protected categories named in HB 132 created intense dissent. As before, the presence of sexual orientation in the list distressed numerous legislators, many of whom were answering to religious constituents who opposed homosexuality. Other lawmakers sought to append new categories to the list. One legislator suggested adding "age including the unborn," an amendment ruled out of order as not germane to the bill. Another addition fared better. Arguing that ranchers needed protection from environmentalist-motivated bias crimes (this was, after all, Wyoming), legislators in the house successfully tacked occupation onto the bill.* Despite all the heat, Bill 132 came the closest to passing of any bias crimes legislation before or since in Wyoming: on third reading, it lost on a thirty-to-thirty tie vote.

---

* Val Pexton tells me that occupation can indeed create tensions. She has seen such tensions in her hometown: "The coal miners have been in Douglas for decades, but they're still treated like crap by the town. They're seen as outsiders." The mining industry is distrusted, creating "the biggest division there"—a division between miners and the rest of town, especially agricultural families. Even though by now plenty of Douglas residents have taken jobs in the mines, miners are still often seen as "transients, squatting there." And even though ranching families may have made money selling out to the mining companies, they often dislike the miners the most.

After the failure of HB 132 in the house, the senate Judiciary Committee killed further discussion of the mirror bill in the senate. Only one bias crimes–related bill remained: HB 193, proposing a "human diversity task force," which had passed the house Judiciary Committee on an eight-to-one vote, and then third reading in the house. But that legislation died in the senate on Friday, February 26th.* Pat Nagel, one of the bill's sponsors, told me that many legislators were simply tired of the whole issue, and Governor Geringer, who had initially suggested the task force, was by late February offering lukewarm support for it at best. Hank Coe, a Republican from Cody and senate majority floor leader, prevented the final bill from reaching the floor for debate, arguing that bias crimes statistics were already compiled in Wyoming under a 1990 federal law. Such stats were indeed being kept, but his objection failed to address the majority of the bill's goals. The bill proposed a five-person task force that would oversee bias crimes training for police officers, study law enforcement's effectiveness in the identification and reporting of bias crimes, and encourage public awareness programs; it would also have required the attorney general to collect and analyze bias crimes data and publish the results annually. It spoke not at all of enhanced penalties; it mentioned no categories of identity, including sexual orientation. It was hard to imagine a bill less controversial. It seemed quite reasonable that some legislators, including Coe, rejected the other bills because they questioned whether the presence of bias necessarily made one crime worthy of more punishment than another, but why oppose legislation that would merely investigate the occurrence of bias crime in Wyoming and encourage its study and prevention? Why indeed?

---

* A week earlier, on February 19th, Billy Jack Gaither, a thirty-nine-year-old gay man, had been beaten to death and burned in Sylacauga, Alabama, by two men. The grandmother of one noted he was "just a typical boy." Commentators on Gaither's murder were quick to note that he didn't flaunt his sexuality, although the killers claimed Gaither came on to them. Despite the many similarities to Matt's murder, Gaither's death failed to attract the same intense degree of attention from the public, the media, the national organizations, and the celebrities that rallied around Matthew.

The answer to that question, and the question of bias crimes legislation's continuing failure in Wyoming, is obviously not simple. Clearly many objections flowed from citizens who opposed any law that even remotely promoted the legitimacy and well-being of gays and lesbians. Those arguments typically proceeded from religious grounds that, while they lacked the reckless viciousness of Fred Phelps's vision, nevertheless unavoidably proceeded from analogous reasoning: homosexuality was a sin, a perversion; to legislate against homophobic bias was tantamount to promoting an anti-Christian agenda. Indeed, the notion that Christians, not gays, were the truly endangered minority drew frequent breath in letters to local papers that year. (Obviously, as evidenced by the Wyoming Church Coalition's support for bias crimes law, not all Wyoming Christians agreed.)

Sometimes, however, the anti-gay sentiment kicked up by the legislation had a more down-home flavor. Legislator Dick Erb— a cosponsor of the 1997 bill outlawing same-sex marriages in Wyoming—told this story about his visit to a Wyoming high school, offering it as an explanation of why gay marriages should be banned: "As I told a group of high school kids," he said, "if you were a rancher and had a gay bull, what would you do with him? One kid said, 'I'd take the sucker to the packing plant.' " Erb recounted this story, according to the Casper *Star-Tribune*, with a chuckle. Such comments might be offhand, but they have a long life—I can think of six local gay and lesbian activists who instantly recalled that tale when I asked them about anti-gay sensibilities in state politics.

Yet homophobia did not lurk beneath every objection to bias crimes legislation. Indeed, some gay rights activists forcefully opposed the diversity task force bill, because they saw it as a watering-down, even a gutting, of legislation that would take a tougher punitive stand on bias crimes. On the other hand, many constituents (myself included), on both the political right and left, gay and straight, were uneasy with the "law and order" sensibility that seemed to drive the call for enhanced penalties; in particular, opponents of the death penalty questioned any legislation that might threaten to increase its use. Such unease was in no way limited to Wyoming; that same year, Queer Watch, an anti–death penalty group based in New York, sharply criticized gay support of bias crimes law. Bill Dobbs, a scathingly funny, brutally direct, and relentless Queer Watch member, also pushed Laramie residents and national gay rights organizations to oppose the death penalty for Matt Shepard's murderers. During a 1999 visit to Laramie, Dobbs cheerfully alienated just about everyone he met, but his single-minded drive paid off: nineteen gay and lesbian organizations across the country, as well as many Wyoming clergy, eventually called for life imprisonment, rather than death, for Henderson and McKinney.

But if Wyoming shared some beliefs with the rest of the nation, it also had its native peculiarities. Wyoming—as Massie and Bob Beck both told me and as a quick scan of any Casper *Star-Tribune* letter page would confirm—just doesn't like passing laws. Period. It wouldn't be entirely fanciful to call that a cowboy thing; more technically, it's a libertarian thing, but whatever you call it, it runs deep here. When the Casper City Council, for example, spent the late 1990s considering an antismoking ordinance, folks wrote letters to the editor suggesting that the ordinance's proponents move to Cuba, or North Korea, or communist China—like-minded totalitarian places, the letters mused. And when the state legislature finally passed a seat belt law in 2000, one lawmaker suggested that the bill moved Wyoming one step closer to becoming a police state. Laws, most any laws, feel like an infringement of personal freedom to many here. When Wyoming faced the loss of millions in federal funds if it didn't outlaw open alcohol containers in automobiles, the state didn't blink: as much as the state could use the money, poor and free (and maybe a bit tipsy, though not illegally so) was better than rich and legislated.

So, more laws seemed at best unnecessary, at worst sinister, to many residents of Wyoming. And in particular, bias crimes law, a few people told me, wouldn't be worth much, simply because bias crimes struck them as a rare event in Wyoming. On the face of it, the numbers seem to back up that opinion: in 1998, for example, Matt's murder was the only bias crime recorded in Albany County. But victims of bias crimes, like victims of rape, often feel intense humiliation and fear retaliation if they report the assault, and, again as in rape, victims of violent bias often assume, rightly or wrongly, that police officers will fail to take them seriously (or, worse, might even agree with the sentiments of the attacker). When victims of bashings are closeted gay men or lesbians, approaching police and testifying in court can feel like an impossible risk. And since reporting bias crimes statistics is voluntary rather than legislatively mandated in Wyoming, it is hard to determine just how uniformly or accurately such crimes are being identified and counted, despite the good will of the local police officers I've encountered.* Altogether, it is hard to know with precision how frequently such violence occurs here, a statistical haziness that further clouds the statewide debate.

However, after more than a year of listening to people's opposition to bias crimes legislation here in Wyoming, it's clear that certain objections have reached the status of mantra: "All crimes are hate crimes." "Murder is murder." "Bias crimes law is thought policing." "Bias crimes law creates special victims and special rights." The premises of some of these mantras are easy to question. For example, it is simply not true that all crimes are hate crimes. The drug dealer and con artist may cause great pain, but their crimes are ones of greed, not hatred. The hit-and-run driver is not motivated by hate; the thief who kills the store clerk is most likely eradicating a potential witness. It would be possible to say that any crime is motivated, on some level, by a fundamental disrespect for social mores, but such disrespect is light-years from bias, from the loathing of certain groups or identities and the decision to act on such loathing.

---

* Bern Haggerty, a Laramie resident and lawyer in the state attorney general's office, has trained police departments around the state in bias crimes identification and investigation. He confirms that official reporting practices in Wyoming are uneven and difficult to track.

I wonder too about the claim "murder is murder." It seems to me that our legal system works on no such assumption. First-degree murder is not involuntary manslaughter, euthanasia is not vehicular homicide, although all these result in the death of another. The drunk driver who hits a bicyclist, the wife who kills her abusive husband in his sleep, the serial killer who stalks his victims, the fired employee who shoots his former boss—these are all killers, but we judge them differently. We consider intent—the drunk driver who accidentally takes a life while his car swerves out of control is culpable in our eyes but not as abhorred as the serial murderer who plans and kills with full knowledge of his wrong-doing. We investigate motive—the abused wife, fearing future assault, who deliberately kills her sleeping husband may be punished but not as severely as the wife who deliberately kills her husband for the insurance money. To me, one of the most compelling aspects of our legal system is this very potential for suppleness—its care for nuance, its desire to differentiate as judiciously as possible among various kinds of criminal acts.

Thus the investigation of motive that bias crimes laws mandate does not seem to me quite the same thing as "thought policing." It is a cherished American right to hold dissenting opinions; it is not a cherished American right to hurt or kill someone on the basis of a dissenting opinion. We punish other actions when we find them to be discriminatory in intent—landlords who refuse to rent to blacks, employers who refuse women jobs or raises—and we punish them not because those punished think blacks or women are inferior but because they act on those beliefs in a way that contravenes the fundamental American principles of equality and freedom (not to mention contravening the concrete freedoms and rights of their victims). To take such questions into consideration when we investigate acts of violence as well doesn't seem to me inconsistent.

That said, I'm not at all sure if the killer of Kristin Lamb, the young Laramie girl murdered in 1998, is any worse an offender than Henderson and McKinney or vice versa; I'm not sure that one or the other deserves worse punishment, "enhanced" penalties. It's hard not to think of severity of punishment as in some way a measure of the value of what has been lost, even though criminal sentencing is driven by many other factors. I think it is that sentiment that angers many opponents of bias crimes law, that natural assumption that the penalty for a crime somehow speaks directly to the "worth" of the victim. In response, it's worth noting that not all bias crimes laws mandate increased penalties; rather, many simply make them available to a judge's or jury's discretion. And supporters of enhanced penalties typically reply as well that bias crimes should be punished more severely because such crimes strike not merely at individual victims but also at entire communities who share the victim's identity and strike as well at America's founding desires for equality and tolerance. Bias crimes laws, they argue, preserve the democratic principle that no one can be deprived of life and liberty simply because he or she belongs to a despised group.

I came to this debate, like many in Wyoming, not having thought about it much before Matt's death. I supported the notion of bias crimes law not because I wanted a law to ensure offenders invariably received more severe punishment but simply to ensure offenders were punished at all: to protect against the possibility that attacking minorities—sexual minorities in particular—couldn't be written off as a justifiable action or a minimally offensive act. Kristen Price and others could then argue all they want that gays "need to be taught a lesson not to come on to straight people"— they just couldn't count on that holding much water in court. Arguments like Price's seem to me haunted by the ugliest excesses of our nation's past, when our courts echoed with similar justifications, similar falsehoods that played on America's most virulent sexual distortions in order to justify acts of discriminatory violence otherwise unjustifiable: black men lynched for their supposed lust, women brutalized for thinking they could venture into the night on their own. Bias crimes legislation like that proposing a human diversity task force would at least disrupt the pernicious logic that gays and lesbians, simply by being gay and lesbian, inflame "understandable" hatreds, should expect their public lives to be greeted with violence. So while I'm uneasy about enhanced penalties, I am certain that I want a police force and legal system that can competently address the undeniable presence of bias in some crimes and that minority groups feel they can trust. And I do want to know, as best as possible, what motivates such crimes—so that we can begin to address them not so much in the penalty phases of criminal trials but back out here, in daily life; so that we can think about ways of heading off such crimes, through education, through better police training, through other kinds of social remedies; so that we can better understand the world we live in and where it goes wrong.

To say all that, of course, acknowledges that while bias crimes law is written in neutral language—"sexual orientation" not "gay," "religion" not "Catholic"—it also tries to answer, for most of its supporters, histories of discrimination in America that have been anything but neutral. That strikes me as the paradox of most any law that addresses discrimination in any form. On the one hand, we want the courts *not* to judge us by our differences. We want the law to abstract us from our gender, our race, our personal identities—to treat all individuals as equals before the law regardless of identity, to see Matt Shepard as simply, neutrally human, for example, and not somehow "less" or "more" of a victim because he was gay. But simultaneously, we want the law to recognize the meaning and substantiality of our differences, to recognize concrete histories of discrimination and prejudice, because without such recognition certain wrongs are much harder to see. The paradox (see me not at all but also see me in full) seems to me inescapable but not paralyzing: we write the law in the language of neutrality, so that whites are as protected as blacks, Christians as protected as Muslims—and then we prove, case by case, the precise realities and concrete specificities of prejudice that underlie each individual incident. That's the best answer I can give to those who fear that any form of bias crimes law invariably creates "special rights" for certain groups: it doesn't. It merely acknowledges the categories of identity that have run through American history like fault lines, and then it pays attention when an individual is denied rights, safety, even life, because someone else deems that individual less equal, less worthy of respect, less human—deems that and then acts violently on such a vision.

59

Chapter Two

To some, the answer to why bias crimes legislation keeps failing in Wyoming has most to do with something else entirely: Wyoming's traditional, even cherished, hostility to outsiders. Mike Massie suggested to me that in 1999, as the nation looked on, the state legislature was more willing to seem "backward" than appear to have bowed to outside pressures to pass a law. And certainly you could hear echoes of that insularity in comments by Governor Geringer after Matt's death, when he announced that Wyoming "can and will deal with this properly on our own. . . . Those who call for a nationally imposed remedy are misdirected" and warned that "there's been too much overreaction by a lot of national organizations." Clearly Geringer's comments (and the reactions of other Wyoming politicians such as Barbara Cubin) derive in part from the familiar antifederal sensibility that suffuses much of the Rocky Mountain West, particularly hard felt in Wyoming, where 49 percent of the state is federal land. But too there's an echo, intended or not, of the West's isolate rough justice, the cowboy's stubborn self-reliance, in statements like the governor's: we'll take care of it ourselves; leave us be.

Val Pexton grew up in the midst of such sentiment. Val wears her red hair cropped short and has a well-honed knack for finding the mordant humor in any situation. She makes quick work of the "cowboy myth" of Wyoming: "That's [mostly] a myth imposed by people who do not live here. There are a few Wyoming people who buy into that, but they're generally not people who grew up on a ranch. [We] weren't cowboys—[we] were people who had cows." But, she says, "Wyoming is a funny place, because there are times when politically it buys into that myth and really tries to put it out there for other people to believe in." State politicians, she has observed, will sometimes act "countrified":

If you accused them of being hicks, they'd be offended, but then they'll turn right around and talk that way. To keep people away, or to keep people from imposing any kind of new land-use regulation, or anything like that. Like the hate crimes legislation when it came around. The kind of noise they were making around that was "we're so simple, we don't need to deal with that," or "you're trying to impose big-city stuff on us. You're trying to impose that stuff that's outside of us on us. We don't let other people impose stuff on us."

A sharp economic irony is at work in such sentiments, according to Val and others, an irony suited to a state that experiences itself as a colony controlled by outside financial interests. Val describes Wyoming as a place dependent on tourist money but resentful of it: "We want people to visit, but we really don't want anyone to stay; and we want them to visit, but we really don't want to have to interact with them; we don't really want to have to cater to them, but we want them to come. And that seems to be the statewide sensibility: we want you to spend your money here, but we don't really want you." Carina Evans echoes Val's point. Carina says her hometown worries hard about how outsiders might see it. In Cheyenne, she laughs, "there's a huge drive to bring in the tourists, bring in the tourists, and you're encouraged to dress western during the summer because that's when the tourists come."

Such self-conscious discomforts aren't exactly new in Wyoming. By the end of the 1920s the state had abolished its board of immigration, choosing to lure tourists rather than settlers, setting the stage for the economic anxieties and pressured performances that today undergird Wyoming's dislike of outsiders. And indeed it can take a long time to become an insider in Wyoming. Folks with a few decades of Wyoming residency under their belt may still be regarded with suspicion; medical practitioners and lawyers—professional types are particularly suspect—are just as likely to advertise how long their families have lived in the state as their alma maters and degrees. And insider status isn't merely granted on the basis of family history. Some might never earn it. When the Lander City Council voted unanimously, barely two weeks after Matt's death, against a resolution to declare the first week of November "Hate Crimes

Awareness Week," one council member argued that "if we do this it will give those people a foot in the door for more laws."* He never clarified exactly who "those people" were, but the intimations were fairly stark nevertheless: whoever they might be, they didn't belong in Lander, at least as part of the public, political process; whoever they might be, the door should stay shut on them.

Lisa and Stephanie of the LGBTA agree that the insider/outsider divide takes on fresh and acute meaning for gays and lesbians in Wyoming. When Lisa first moved from Fort Collins to attend the university here, she "wanted to feel like Laramie could be home." "Testing out the waters," she began to believe that "yeah, maybe this is going to be okay." But soon after her arrival, as she worked parking lots for her university police job, she'd see bumper stickers with messages like "Welcome to Wyoming. Have a Nice Trip Home" or "I don't give a damn how you did it back home, this is Wyoming." Lisa says her first response was simply to think, "Yo, shit, settle down there. But then you wonder. If that's how you treat visitors to your state, prospective citizens, prospective businesses. . . ." She leaves her last question implied: if that's how you treat them, then how are you going to treat me?

Stephanie, born and raised in Wyoming, sums up her experience of the political atmosphere for gay life in the state: "There is a tremendous xenophobia here. Wyoming is run—now not everybody here is like this—but Wyoming is *run* by people who have a great deal invested in making sure nothing changes. And that includes civil rights. And that includes people like Lisa and myself."

---

* He also had a concise and remarkably familiar objection to hate crimes legislation: "Murder is murder, assault is assault. I just have a real problem with more laws" (Casper *Star-Tribune*, October 30, 1998, p. B1).

CHAPTER THREE

I'm seeing the title for this chapter that we're
going to become in Beth's book: it's going to be
called "Dear God, They Got Queers!"
—Lisa

Any way you slice it, it isn't easy to be gay in Wyoming. In a state of less than five hundred thousand people, there isn't a single gay bar, bookstore, or permanent, public gathering place; and in such a rural and sparsely populated region, talking about the closet means something quite different when there are simply very few places to be outside of it. Historians of gay life have argued that the opportunities for anonymity that accompanied the rise of urban life in America have been precious to the formation of gay and lesbian identities and communities—as Joe, a member of the United Gays and Lesbians of Wyoming told me, the wonderful thing about cities is that "you can get lost in the crowd, but you can also find yourself in the crowd." In Wyoming, where crowds are an unlikely phenomenon, finding yourself as a gay person can be tricky indeed. That matters deeply for lesbian and gay individuals here, and it matters as well for the politics of sexuality in Wyoming, a state where many still manage to greet the notion of gay residents with mild disbelief.

Or worse. While the great majority of the letters I've seen— written to Wyoming papers and to the LGBTA—deplored Matt's death, it would be a lie to say the murder summoned forth only expressions of sympathy and tolerance. One letter, published in the Casper *Star-Tribune* the week after Matt's death, described Matt as an "unfortunate person" who had "cheated disease" by being murdered; yet another that same day angrily began, "We are sick and tired of all the whoopla about a homosexual's death," and deemed homosexuality "immoral and disgusting." Five minutes into a conversation about sexuality with just about any Wyoming resident, gay or straight, you'll invariably hear the statewide script: "Wyoming is a 'live and let live' kind of place—we don't get into other people's business." But gay and lesbian residents will add a crucial coda: It's live and let live, all right, except when it comes to homosexuality. Then, as one gay man told me, "It's more like, you don't tell us you're gay, and we won't exile you or hurt you." Chad, a gay undergraduate at UW, says Wyoming has a "don't ask, don't tell" mentality: "People don't ask, and they don't expect you to tell them either. Which I guess you could say is either a positive or a negative. [You could think], okay, it doesn't really matter, when in actuality it really does. It may seem superficially positive, but deep down it's really, really negative. Very, very bad for some people." He knew of a gay couple in Sheridan, his hometown, who decided to have a commitment ceremony, which actually appeared in the newspaper's wedding announcements. But he's also seen local people take out ads in the paper denouncing gay marriage as "against God" and a "one-way ticket to hell." "It's very, very depressing." As one letter writer to the *Star-Tribune* told gay residents, Wyoming is "not San Francisco": "You should stick with your own and keep it under your hat."

Not all straight residents of the state feel that way, of course; some have thought hard about the difficulties of gay life here. Val Pexton remembers a man from her hometown of Douglas who began cross-dressing as a woman. People threatened him, threw things at him, beat him. "He had a lot of guts," she says. "Unfortunately, the truth about Wyoming is, where I'm from anyway, and I find it here too, they really don't want you to be very different. They like to pretend we're all the same." Carina Evans seconds that point. Even in Cheyenne, the home base of United Gays and Lesbians of Wyoming, she has witnessed "a real discomfort with gay people in general. They just don't want to know, don't want to deal with it." The results of such discomfort are rarely the kind of violence visited upon Matt, but the effects, in daily life, are corrosive nonetheless. Back in Douglas, Val knew a lesbian couple who "were fine, as long as they pretended like they were roommates." Once they grew tired of the pretense, simply wanted to be a couple, life changed. One of the two, a schoolteacher, encountered harassment from her students and their parents—not violent threats, Val says, but certainly a "general nastiness." Val's reinterpretation of the "live and let live" principle goes like this: "If you just would quit stirring people up and making them hate you, we could get along." Of course, "stirring up" can mean something as simple as merely acknowledging you're not straight. If you're gay, that doesn't always leave you much room to breathe.

For some writers, Matt's murder offered a window on something quite different: the question and experience of heterosexual masculinity. JoAnn Wypijewski took up that investigation in *Harper's Magazine*, postulating that Matt might have died not because he was gay but because Henderson and McKinney were straight, were burdened by the fear of "wussitude." A version of that argument got made locally as well, by K. C. Compton, editor of the Casper *Star-Tribune*, who felt the killers drew their lethal intensity from "the terror of being a sissy." Such arguments struck a resounding chord in the literature classroom of University of Wyoming professor Bonnie Zare; her students, assigned the *Harper's* essay in the spring of 1999, freely and sympathetically enumerated the heavy pressures facing young men, the risks of seeming less than fully masculine, the emotional shutdown that strikes them as the high but necessary cost of manhood. Clearly those pressures have a burdensome existence, particularly during the difficult passage from boy to man; but in this case I feel uneasy around such arguments, not because they identify what strikes me as a real truth about the often ill-fitting and anxious contours of contemporary masculinity but because they nudge up against the possibility of cheap psychologizing or quick and dirty cultural theorizing. They nudge up against a certain forgetfulness about that night on the prairie. Neither Compton nor Wypijewski slides down that slippery slope, but the risk is there: the empty flourishing of explanatory terms, the chanting of generic motives, magical talismans that offer us at best only the opportunity to begin thinking about that night and at worst the allure and comforts of fraudulent knowingness.

In the early months of my research, I spent some time describing my thoughts to a colleague, who replied, "I see you'll be talking about homophobia—will you be discussing heterosexism too?" And I remembering thinking, with a certain impatience: Jesus. We make that move too easily—that move from the narrow strip of fence where Matt died to the big cultural and political weather fronts grinding along overhead. That move is necessary, I think, if we want to change that weather, but the trip should be hard, something we can't map out easily in advance. Because neither homophobia nor heterosexism tied Matt to that fence: Henderson and McKinney did. They weren't murdering the "wuss within" that night—they were murdering Matt.

Most people outside Wyoming in any case might find it surprising to consider us hard up for serious manhood, given the cowboy romance of the place. Max Ember, a Hollywood screenwriter who called me up a year after the murder for information about the case, seemed genuinely nonplussed that Wyoming boys like McKinney and Henderson could be so, well, short. (I seem to remember that he summed up his screenplay's theme as "the story of three boys in macho-macho land.") Or take another example, a good friend of mine from California who stopped for gas while driving through Wyoming. At the station she noticed a man dressed in a cowboy hat, boots, and Wrangler jeans and thought, "Wow, look at that. He isn't afraid to be out at all." Then she realized he wasn't a gay man indulging in the cowboy look—

he really was a cowboy. The possibilities of masculinity don't run as narrow as all that here, but the expectations of conventional manhood are clearly felt nonetheless. I ran into them both—the pressing boundaries and the recognition of their restrictiveness—one day at the Spic and Span Laundromat in Laramie, a few months after the murder. A twenty-something young man, wiry and thin, was there, doing what looked to me like two months' worth of laundry. He wouldn't let me use his name, but he nevertheless struck me as indigenously frank. He'd been "roughneck-ing" for the past year, working oil well sites, and had come to Laramie for a change of pace and maybe in a year or two some training in car repair at Wyo Tech, a local school. He told me he doesn't like gays but that in his opinion Matt didn't deserve what happened to him: "Those guys are assholes, beating on someone so small." I asked him if he would react violently if a gay man approached him; he replied, "Well, I wouldn't like it, but if he were smaller than me, I'd just tell him to leave. I wouldn't hit him." What if he were bigger than you, I asked? For the first and only time in our conversation he cracked a grin. "Well, I guess I wouldn't hit him either."

The impulse in the analysis of Matt's death has been to char-acterize Wyoming as either utterly different—a more backward, more primitive "cowboy culture"—or just like the rest of Amer-ica. The former is not merely the product of coastal chauvinism—a popular state slogan trumpets that Wyoming is "What America Once Was," a touristy nostalgia that feeds such regional snob-beries (and whose meaning, in the aftermath of Matt's death, slides unintentionally into something far darker). Regional stereotyping of that sort doesn't get one anywhere in understand-ing the murder's context, but some truths are lost as well if we swing completely to the other side and claim Laramie and Wyoming are no different from the rest of America when it comes to the experience of sexual identity. But if this region has its dis-tinctiveness, it is not because John Wayne still walks tall here. The distinction is more elusive than that, and it is not one you'll find by talking to straight residents of the state. It seems to me that you can indeed take the murder as an opportunity to clarify the injuries of straight masculinity, the fearful dodging of sissyhood; but it seems to me too that what that night asks of us, far more urgently, is a fresh understanding of gay life rather than simply gay death.

※

"If you don't admit that Matthew made a mistake in that bar that night, you can't understand the big picture of being gay in Wyoming," Jim, a gay man from Cheyenne, tells me. I'm sitting with him and his partner, Travis, behind Coal Creek Coffee one night in July, the freight trains rolling past a few dozen feet away. They're a striking couple, alternately funny and intense. "There was no place for Matt to go and be gay, be out, be comfortable," Jim adds. Mark, a gay man who grew up on a ranch near Cheyenne, says something similar when I talk to him later that summer: "I don't think that Matthew Shepard kept the way he was hidden, which I think, for Laramie, took an awful lot more guts than I ever had. I know that bar, I wouldn't have gone in there. And I think I'm a little better capable of physically defending myself than the average person." The tone of these comments is difficult to capture: saddened, certainly, and with a hint of head-shaking admiration for Matt's naive openness. But you can also hear the frustration that comes with having been forced to study the perimeter of your own safety.

That guardedness is something of a way of life for many of the gay men and lesbians I've met in Laramie. They don't feel like victims and, in the lives they've made here, certainly couldn't be understood as such. But still you'd lose something of the texture of their lives if you failed to acknowledge the background hum of calculation, the daily quick math that accompanies gay life, where each act of openness must be weighed against the potential friends, acquaintances, jobs, happiness lost. That arithmetic is harder when it's unrelieved, as it usually is in Wyoming—where there are few places, beyond circles of trusted friends or small, geographically distant organizations, to be out without pause or second-guessing. Laramie and Cheyenne, home to the LGBTA and the UGLW, lie in the southeastern corner of Wyoming, geographically closer to the gay communities in Denver and Fort Collins. That accident of location makes them something of a gay haven compared to the rest of the state—as Chad puts it, "The good thing about Laramie is that you've got easy escape to Colorado." John Little, executive director and former president of the UGLW, used to reside in the small Wyoming towns of Wamsutter and Riverton and has lived the comparison: "It's a whole different world out there. You're very much alone out there. You might have maybe two or three other gay and lesbian friends, but that's about it. There's a lot of people very, very in the closet." In Riverton, John lived with his partner. "When we were in Riverton, we were pretty much 'out,' and there were a lot of [gay] people who had nothing to do with us." They feared, John says, a certain guilt by association—a common quandary, other gay residents tell me. Jim, for example, knows some gay men in Gillette who want to organize a social group but are stymied by their fear of parking outside each other's houses, and John tells me that some gay men he knows in small towns have been afraid to rent gay-themed films—even the most innocuous fare, like *The Birdcage*—at mom-and-pop video stores. At UW, some gay and lesbian faculty and staff have been reluctant to openly associate with each other or with the LGBTA for fear it might rebound on their tenure decisions. The smaller the town, the more pronounced such isolation is, John Little remembers. "There is no anonymity. . . . [There was] never any violence directed at me or anyone I knew of—but more than anything an overwhelming feeling of intense isolation. I lived in Wamsutter eight years: every weekend I had off I hit the road on Friday night and headed down to Fort Collins and Denver. I didn't know there was any gay community in Wyoming—I couldn't find it."

Talk to gay men here, and you can begin to draw a secret map of Wyoming, one most of its residents would find unfamiliar. There are the particular rest stops and scenic overlooks on certain highways where men can find fleeting companionship; the Cheyenne drag clubhouse without a liquor license that had a short, heady life in the early 1990s; the town parks in Powell and Lander that turn "cruisy" at night; and The Fort, an adult book and video store south of Laramie with private viewing booths and (as one Web guide to gay Wyoming puts it) "friendly and professional management." Spend some time at cruisingforsex.com on the Web, and you can find the Wyoming message board, a rather lonely site compared to the heavy traffic on the other state boards. In the Wyoming room, the conversation seems to be mostly among men from out of state, guys with anatomically impressive online handles who are jetting into Jackson for a few days of skiing and sex—talk about colonization—with the occasional plaintive interruption from a local, wondering where all the gay Wyomingites are. As Travis put it that night at Coal Creek, there is plenty of gay sex happening in Wyoming—it's a steady flow of public community and companionship that is much harder to find.

I've had long conversations with more than a dozen gay men for this book, and each has echoed Travis: friendship, companionship, and community can be much more difficult to discover than sex. And each has linked that truth to the intensities of isolation, the widespread hiddenness, of gay life in the rural landscapes of Wyoming. (None of them, unsurprisingly, sees the occurrence of anonymous sex as some perverse essence of gay biology, no matter how often the religious right tells them so.) Too, it's the ability to express affection in the most simple of ways—a touch on the shoulder, a quick kiss goodbye—that gay men in Wyoming seem to long for most and find most impossible, feel they must always shut down. It is expressions of affection, not sex, that strike them as most threatening to whatever harsh codes of masculinity still linger here and are therefore most dangerous—another kind of guardedness that sharpens the already hard edge of Wyoming's solitude.

But in the last few years what has begun to transform that isolation, in fascinating and dramatic fashion, is the Internet. If each gay man I've spoken to for this book has experienced the loneliness of coming out in Wyoming, each has also found deep and unexpected connections online. Travis, Jim, and Chad all tell me that the opportunity for online contact and conversation has profoundly changed their lives, opening new territories for information sharing, friendship, and romance, exponentially increasing their social worlds (at least two men I interviewed had also met Matt online—even on the Net, Wyoming is a small place). The Internet has also radically transformed the nature of coming out. The story of Mike, a UW grad student and active member of the LGBTA, could serve as a blueprint.

Mike, in his thirties, is a compact, reserved man who has spent his life in the rural landscapes of America; born in Illinois, he arrived in Laramie in 1996. Mike's coming-out began only shortly before his move here and is still, he readily admits, a work in progress (when I flip on my tape recorder the day we talk, Mike leans over it and waves: "Hi, Mom, Hi, Dad"). "I had always known that I was curious about men, but I didn't really understand what that curiosity, what that attraction was. I grew up on a farm in the Midwest, and the only images, the only information about gay men was it was a man that wanted to be a woman, acted like a woman. I had no role models of any 'masculine' gay men. It was all about being effeminate." Mike was, and still clearly is, deeply troubled by that vision of homosexuality. "So this attraction for men—the best I could come up with was that I had a poor self-image, and I would see these men and want to be like them."

If there were gay men in Mike's hometown, he didn't know of them, and homosexuality, he says, was barely discussed and if so never with anything beyond swift disgust or mockery—certainly not with frankness or openness (a truth—perhaps a particularly rural one—echoed by Travis and Mark, both sons of Wyoming ranch families, and by Jim Osborn, who remembers the thrill of finding a definition of homosexuality in an old high school library book). Mike would find his illumination elsewhere. "It wasn't until probably five years ago that the Internet started becoming really used. [Gay] people were putting up Web pages. And actually, by accident, I came across a site with links to a whole bunch of different gay men who were this masculine role model—the 'bear' subculture" of gay men, who cultivate a rugged, bearded, masculine style. Mike smiles in bemusement: "I was looking for information about grizzly bears, and I find these guys. I thought wow—that's what I am. At least it started that process of growth." By the time Mike moved to Laramie, he was taking his first, apprehensive steps into online conversation. "I was really nervous at first to go into some gay chat rooms." He told online contacts, " 'Well, you know, I'm curious.' And I made friends on there that are going to be lifelong friends."

Those friendships and connections slowly moved offline for Mike, as he began to date. "Six months or so after that I decided that this was something I actually wanted to try and experience. I picked out a guy who had one of the first Web pages that I saw, wrote back and forth with him. He was several states away. We visited once and just basically had dinner, then continued to email and went back for a [second] visit. It was a great visit." But still Mike felt the deeper intensities of living as a gay man in the real world, not simply the virtual one. "After that, it was a process of coming to grips, for myself, with [what it meant]. I still had these notions of gay being equated with feminine, and that was quite a long process, to go through that, that I am not less of a man because of my sexuality. That took a long time." He feels troubled too, "because I can pass as heterosexual. I feel guilty about that sometimes, because I've heard people receive compliments—'you don't act gay'—which is intended as a compliment, but when you think about it, it's like, oh, you don't get it. That was nice of you to say, but you don't get it. The drag queens have done a tremendous amount of work in advancing gay rights, while the rest of us are just kind of passing and have quiet lives, not making waves." And Mike has felt more general stigmas as well, confronting "all the issues of I'm not a bad person, even though that's what society [says]."

Laramie, despite the isolations of Wyoming, has not been a complete hindrance to Mike's coming-out. "It's been good and bad. It's good because I'm not really immersed in the scene of the big-city gay life, which I've been exploring quite a bit in Denver. . . . That life is easy for people to really get trapped into what I would call the gay lifestyle." Mike says he doesn't usually use that term but feels it captures some aspects of gay life he remains uncomfortable with:

Promiscuity, dissatisfaction . . . searching for Mr. Right but also for Mr. Right Now . . . all the emotion turmoil that that causes. I see a lot of pain down there, and a lot of people that are really searching for something, but they don't know what they're looking for, and they go for the quick fix of some kind of sexual encounter . . . going to the bars, the whole cruising thing. It's pretty unsettling. It's been fun for me at first to get the attention, but it's not a healthy kind of attention, which has recently come into clear focus.

For Mike, "Living in Laramie shielded me from that, because I have to make an effort to go to Denver, so I'm not immersed in that culture all the time." But he does long for other aspects of urban gay culture—discussion series, book groups, coffeehouses, the public world of gay socializing. "I have mixed feelings about living here. But the fear of getting sucked into that scene holds me back."

Mike, like so many gay men I've spoken to here, has fashioned a life out of seemingly incommensurate materials, out of the quiet, hard edges of Wyoming and the vaporous, streaming sociality of high technology. But it's crucial to remember that such an opposition is not clear-cut, that the online world is no utopia of absolute openness, no perfect respite. One summer morning, Chad met me in the university library's computer room and cheerfully guided me through a few chat rooms run by Gay.com and the UGLW. As we laughed at some of the more inflated handles, Chad explained that online conversants "always put what they call their 'stats' on there—their age, height, weight, hair color, usually how 'big' they are." He showed me a particularly stupendous example and flicked up an eyebrow: "Okay— that's supposed to be impressive why?" While we surfed, Chad revealed what he experiences as the less savory side of online community. He has made some good friends through the Net, "but there's also a large percentage of married people, which is very, very weird. A lot of them want to talk," but more often, Chad bemoaned, they are seeking something else. They might ask, "Will you hook up with me?" Chad seemed genuinely disturbed by this notion: "God no!" He gets such folks off his back quickly (usually by asking if they want their wives to be there too), but still such encounters clearly make him deeply uncomfortable.

Other gay men confirm Chad's observation, that many gay men online are married, in families, living lives of complete disguise relieved only by fleeting contacts online, contacts that often are primarily focused on arranging offline sexual encounters. Larz, a UW graduate student in his early forties, became friends with Chad online; he too echoes Chad's unease, frustrated that the promise of virtuality has not evaporated the strictures of the closet. But Larz—like Travis, Jim, Mike, and Chad—still believes in the possibility of establishing trust online. Travis and Jim point out that you create that trust slowly, over a series of online conversations, gauging, usually by degree of detail, how open and candid a correspondent is in response to personal questions; and Chad—who tells me that most of his online friendships remain on the Net—notes that if you do meet someone face to face, "You meet in a very public place. It's usually very, very public."

Mike would concur with them: "The Internet continues to be a really important tool for meeting people, and I find that for me anyway it's very effective. I'm able to have a typewritten conversation with someone, and by not being face to face it really removes a lot of the tension that is really heavy in a bar-type situation. The Internet removes that, and you can have a much deeper conversation online." Mike feels too that, ironically, the anonymities of the Net actually create the opportunity for richer intimacy (and forestall the nameless sexual encounters that characterize one version of gay life he wishes to avoid): "The fact that you're not anywhere near each other removes the temptation to meet in person right away, so you can have these discussions spaced out over a period of time. I've found that I can ask some really deep questions, and I can judge the answers really well. Either people will come back with really deep answers, or they'll be shallow. It sorts people out."

Mike's trust has yet to be betrayed online: "I have not had a bad experience. I've met people where we didn't hit it off—we had a good online rapport but in person there was no chemistry. But I haven't had anyone be radically different from what I expected." He attributes his good fortune to the care he takes online. "There are a few lessons to learn on the Internet," he tells me. "One is don't build expectations—take them as they are, don't build them up in your mind. Be patient, don't try to rush things. And probably the number one rule is don't take things personally. In general that's a rule for dating in person too." Mike, who is often quite solemn in appearance, begins to laugh. "But I missed all that. In high school I didn't date; I think a girl asked me to the prom, but it wasn't a date. I didn't date in college. I was a workaholic all through my twenties, not really understanding myself. In many ways I'm a teenager again. I would hope that I'm working through it faster than a teenager would, but still I'm having to go through all that." Grinning, he tells me that he often feels like "the proverbial schoolgirl, all nervous and jittery." But despite the nerves, you can see how deep Mike's happiness now runs: "It's been quite a trip, but life is so, so much better now that I have an understanding of myself. I'm a whole person now. It's a wonderful thing."

If it sounds like a certain sexual conservatism runs through the stories above, it would be wrong to think you'd find nothing else here. Mark—the third-generation Cheyenne ranch son—would make quick work of such simple assumptions. Mark, who spent several years in Laramie, now lives in northern Colorado. We met at a diner near Fort Collins, and Mark, wearing a baseball cap and T-shirt, looked like he could have hopped out of any one of the pickups parked outside the restaurant. Mark says he was "introverted" as a kid: "I liked the ranch, and I had no problems with the work, I liked the freedom." But intellectually and socially, "it didn't offer a lot. . . . There were no kids my age [on the ranch], there was none within walking distance. To be with somebody your age was a special occasion." Still, Mark laughs at the thought that such an upbringing could only result in an unsophisticated hick. He tells a story about a 4-H trip he took while a teenager, during which he ironically played to the snobbery of the out-of-state students he met by expressing shock at hotel-room phones:

"You mean you don't have to walk to the country store?" He shakes his head at the memory.

Mark, who graduated from high school in 1983, didn't come out until college. "I can look back now and realize that the way I looked at men would be gay . . . but where I was raised it was wrong, it was unnatural. . . . I went to real extremes to keep it hidden. I wasn't picked on in school; I was called queer or fag, but it never felt to me like they knew, it was more a general insult. I tried to minimize being different, and I think that was not because of the way I felt but because if I showed myself to be different people would zero in . . . and I didn't know what I felt." He remembers coming out to himself—acknowledging to himself that he was gay—while an undergraduate at UW: "I admit I cried that night, because I was so scared of AIDS, I'm never going to fit in to society, I can't act how I want. . . . But then I went, that's a stupid attitude." Mark found little to draw him to the LGBTA; it struck him as cliquish, and he steered clear. After graduating with a degree in psychology, Mark kicked around in a variety of blue-collar jobs and then found his current career. Smack in the middle of Laramie, Mark became a sexual entrepreneur. He became a partner in a mail-order business in what he calls "the gay fetish area," selling cowboy boots and gear to places as far-flung as Japan (Laramie, he tells me, has invaluable cachet as a catalog address in such a business). Mark has also dabbled in phone sex and video production and publishes several gay pornographic magazines, including, perhaps inevitably, *Cowpokes.*

Mark and his partner have since moved their business to Colorado (shortening the drive to Denver, where they regularly replenish their fetish supplies). But Mark doesn't see Wyoming as necessarily a place to flee. "You don't have to deny who you are" in Wyoming—"I think you just have to be really careful. You have to choose who you're going to be around, you're going to have to choose, if you're going to act in that capacity, where you do it and how you do it a little better than you would in a major metropolitan area. I will act differently in New York City, and I will act differently in Denver, and I will act differently in L.A., and I will act differently in San Francisco. Because I know what is tolerated there." There is indeed a certain limited visibility to the life he describes, but the life still exists, even flourishes, and as the stories of Mike, Mark, and others might intimate, the routes to gay identity and companionship in Wyoming are blazed every day, in ways many and unexpected.

The stories above are ones deeply shaped by isolation, but gay and lesbian organizations are beginning to lay a network of gay sociability and activism across the state. The UGLW—founded in the late 1980s—and the LGBTA are probably the most visible gay and lesbian groups in Wyoming, but not the only ones. Casper College houses an active Safe Zone project that promotes gay tolerance; several Parents, Family, and Friends of Lesbians and Gays (PFLAG) groups meet around the state; the Wyoming Grassroots Project (with local chapters in several counties) includes gay issues and gay and lesbian members in its agitation for human rights; at least one informal, unnamed group gathers regularly in Fremont County and invites new members through a listing in the UGLW's newsletter. Community Outreach for Prevention and Education (COPE), an AIDS organization in Casper, also plans dances several times a year for gay and lesbian socializing. The HIV/AIDS Resource and Training (HART) Center in Cheyenne, another HIV/AIDS prevention organization, shares its office space with the UGLW, runs an LGBT youth group, and eagerly supports gay and lesbian issues. The Wyoming Aids Project administers The Tree House, a small but devoted center for people living with HIV/AIDS. But even the AIDS prevention network—in the 1980s particularly the tough, resilient backbone of much gay organizing throughout America—is fragile in Wyoming. When I tried to reach the Albany County AIDS Project here in Laramie I got an answering machine message that didn't even mention the organization by name and instead warned that all calls to that line were screened. Housed at Planned Parenthood, it's understandable that ACAP might be wary of crank calls or worse, but it is difficult to imagine calling that line as someone closeted and just diagnosed. The project also struggles on a truly shoestring budget—several UW Greek houses held a 1999 fund-raiser barbecue simply to ensure that ACAP could afford a post office box.

The Albany County AIDS Project might be so broke, Peggy Hutchings, director of the HART center in Cheyenne, tells me, because AIDS simply isn't on the daily radar in Wyoming. Like many living in rural regions of the United States, most Wyoming residents assume AIDS is an urban disease, nothing to worry about here. As Peggy points out, such assumptions, married to the deeply closeted lives many gay and bisexual men lead in Wyoming, can create serious conditions of risk; add the disbelief in local contagion to the likelihood of anonymous encounters, and you can understand Peggy's fervent commitment to safe-sex education. Peggy, a married, middle-aged woman, is an entrancing contradiction in terms: she has the chipper, can-do spirit and no-nonsense grooming of a suburban mom, casserole recipes and carpool schedules at her fingertips; at the same time, she talks knowledgeably and freely about dental dams and anal sex. Seated in her wicker-filled office at the HART Center—a comfortably decorated cottage submerged in bushes on the edge of a Cheyenne city park—we talk about her work, which includes educating local youth—lesbians, gays, bisexuals, and transgenders in particular—about safe sex. She has worked at the balancing act; after a few minutes, you can easily imagine her handing out condoms with the Sunny Delight.

As Peggy will tell you, AIDS, despite local disregard, has indeed arrived in Wyoming. To her, the founding of the HART Center in 1994 (then just a hotline and information clearinghouse) was long overdue. In 1999, according to the Wyoming Department of Health, nine HIV infections and fourteen people with AIDS were reported statewide; since it began documenting cases in 1984, the Health Department has counted a total of 173 AIDS diagnoses, of which 96 involved gay men. To anyone outside Wyoming those numbers probably seem remarkably small, and even given Wyoming's sparse population, officially calculated rates of infection are fairly low here. But AIDS cases are probably undercounted in Wyoming (although not catastrophically). Some patients, Peggy speculates, might seek diagnosis and treatment in Colorado or other neighboring states, away from small-town prying. And since few residents—gay and straight alike—believe AIDS has penetrated the state borders, it's likely that Wyoming has a number of undiagnosed cases. Still, even adjusting for potential misses, the actual, rather than statistical, tally of AIDS cases in Wyoming, widely dispersed geographically, doesn't make for the critical mass that might galvanize gay activism. It's one reason, it seems to me, that activists I've met outside Wyoming can look at the state and bemoan the seeming lack of indigenous gay politicking.

But such censure I think also misses the point. The UGLW and other gay groups, both formal and informal, do indeed focus much of their energies on social events rather than more obviously "political" activities—planning dances, coffeehouses, and parties for their members, as well as larger events such as The Rendezvous, a multiday camping extravaganza organized annually by the UGLW that draws over three hundred participants from Wyoming and neighboring states. At first glance, such efforts might appear politically trivial, certainly not "activist" in the most rigorous sense of the word: it's easy to wonder what the long-term impact of party throwing might be. But in the context of Wyoming—a state defined by its utter lack of public places for gay and lesbian gathering—those social events are profoundly important in creating and nurturing gay and lesbian community and safety and providing escape from the loneliness and invisibility that characterize so much gay life in the Rocky Mountain West. Stephanie, of the LGBTA, describes Wyoming as something of a "moon settlement": "I think it is possible to be happy here and be queer. It's just easier to do it anywhere else." Groups like the LGBTA, she says, make the difference.

While lesbian women in Wyoming experience many of the same trials as gay men do, their social networks are typically concrete rather than online. In our conversation, Stephanie speculated that as a woman she might in particular seek such communities, not because of any "feminine essence" but because women are "socialized more than men, so community is an option." Still,

Stephanie says, if there is anything like a gay and lesbian community in Laramie, "it's a community that doesn't have a big social presence and doesn't have much of an awareness of itself as a defined entity. There's not a feeling of unity. You can't point and say, that's the gay part of Laramie." In particular, Stephanie tells me, "I'm not sure there is a true [lesbian] community, because there's a lot of divides. . . . There's a split in age, I've noticed. There's a whole lesbian community of which I have never been a part because I am a student. I don't mean that they deliberately exclude the younger set, and I don't think that the younger set deliberately excludes people who are a little older, [but] nobody's willing to bridge that gap." Renné, a lesbian student in the LGBTA, seconds Stephanie's observation, saying Laramie's lesbian community seems "segregated agewise" and describing her wish for mentoring from older lesbians. Still, she laughs, there's always a lesbian potluck to attend.

When we met, Renné was planning a career in law enforcement and training seriously for the physical tests she would have to pass. With short black hair and a taste for movies like *GI Jane*, she might fit the assumption I've heard from several gay men, who believe life in Wyoming must be easier for lesbians, since the outdoorsy, ranchwoman look is so common here. Renné laughs at the thought and tells me it's not really true. She echoes a story I've heard from other Wyoming lesbians, that when a lesbian arrives in Wyoming it might first look like butch heaven—but while lesbian women might have a little more room to breathe, it would be a mistake to think their lives are all that different from the lives of gay men here. Still, Renné really likes Laramie: "It's such a great little town." While she does think gay people here are isolated, "the potential is there. It's all right here."

Mary Jane Trout, a lesbian women who moved to Laramie a few years back, knows where the real utopia is. Mary Jane has an irrepressibly warm personality and a juicy Texan accent to go with it (she tells me she was "born and raised in the Middle of Nowhere, Texas"). She lived in the Bay Area in the 1970s, and "it was like heaven for me. When you can look in the phone book and go to a lesbian mechanic, or you can call a lesbian plumber, and you can go to a lesbian dance where there are five hundred lesbians and half of them have kids and there's child care provided . . . that is political excitement." Mary Jane remembers being "full of fire" then—she participated in consciousness-raising groups, helped to set up a women's center in a small community near San Francisco, and engaged in serious antiwar activism. "I used to be out there on the front lines getting teargassed," she recalls with nostalgia. Mary Jane came through America's first wave of gay and lesbian activism: "Back then people didn't really connect, who were gay or lesbian, with their community. Some of them probably didn't know what that meant."

In a sense, moving to Laramie has meant a repeat of that first wave. She has found a sociable lesbian community here (one that stays in touch frequently through a private email list), but it is small and only partly in view: "Because they're afraid. It's one thing to go to a party at someone's house, but it's another thing to go to one of the LGBTA meetings and be more openly involved, whichever age group you're in" (indeed, Mary Jane asked to use a pseudonym because her partner is a junior professor, and they both worry that full openness could hurt her chances at tenure). Mary Jane agrees with Stephanie and Renné, saying she'd like to build connections between older and younger lesbians. She doesn't think that would be all that hard, that simple social encounters could make the difference. She talks about a young woman she saw one day, wearing a gay pride shirt. Mary Jane told her, "I've been a lesbian longer than you've been alive. That really tickled her—she was so happy."

To Mary Jane, "Laramie isn't that different from anywhere else. Maybe in degrees, but that's it. It's certainly not that different from Texas. And if you see how many gay bashings have happened in San Francisco, it's not that different, especially when it comes to physical safety." The difference lies in the ease of emotional well-being for gays and lesbians and its link to public, social opportunities: "I think that emotional well-being comes from within," Mary Jane says, but for those just coming to terms with their sexuality, "there are places where it's much easier to develop that emotional safety, [like] when you're in a large community like San Francisco. I think it's very hard to develop it without that. But once you have it, you have it, and you can take it anywhere."

The UGLW, LGBTA, and other gay groups have continued to provide such crucial social opportunities since Matt's death, but his murder has also catalyzed a transformation, and often a turn to political activism, among many gay residents of the state. Most of the gay men and lesbians I have spoken to feel that gay residents either came further out in the murder's aftermath or, as Chad put it, "went screaming back into the closet." Chad, who says he felt "uncomfortable but never afraid" after the murder, had come out only shortly before Matt's death; while he steered clear of the LGBTA that year (simply, he says, out of an aversion for joining groups), he has increasingly focused his academic work on gay studies. John Little of the UGLW thinks "more people have come out since Matt died—[it] has had that effect. Some people came out in the heat of the moment and then looked around and said, hmm, where am I . . . and some have rejoiced in it, and some have stepped back." Travis and Jim took such steps, although they tell me it was for them caused less by a conscious political choice on their part and more by the simple fact that talk about homosexuality had increased. People felt the need to pay at least "lip service to tolerance," Travis says, and that created opportunities for coming out.

Larz's decision was more overtly political, although not traditionally activist. He decided to move to Laramie and attend graduate school at UW only after the murder. "Matt did affect my decision to come here. I thought, it's more important than ever for me to be myself here in Laramie. It's more important than ever to make a statement about being [gay] without carrying a banner. I can do more good by going to Wal-Mart and saying hi to a mother and her child than I ever could carrying a placard outside Wal-Mart saying 'Diversity Now.'" Indeed, while clearly gay activism has had a much larger presence in state politics since Matt's death—consider the bias crimes debate alone—such moves to political agitation have not always been easy. Or welcome. John Little points out that membership in the UGLW, around 175 dues-paying members before the attack, "jumped up pretty good right after Matt's murder, but then it has dwindled back down. We're still over the 200 mark, but at one time we were up around 230, 250. People got very interested, but then the intensity fell away." He thinks the political urgency felt by many after the murder faded, "because the bias crimes law didn't pass, so a lot of people threw up their hands in frustration." But he also attributes the decline in membership to a discomfort with politics in general. "Some of the feedback we've been getting is that some folks tend to view UGLW as a social organization, but over the course of the past year we've tried to become a bit more activist oriented, and the social side has suffered. So [there has been] a little alienation. We're trying hard to find a good balance." And the UGLW's support for bias crimes legislation has angered some of its more conservative members, John says—"I never met a gay Republican until I moved to Wyoming." But "as hard as it's been, it has actually taken UGLW in a direction that it needed to go. It's forced the issue to help us transition from a few social events a year into something that can step out into the forefront for the gay community. There really is a pretty good gay population here, it's just a bit under the surface. I know there is."

Mike feels that the murder has been "woven into his coming-out process"—he has come out not merely as a gay man but also as an activist. He began attending LGBTA meetings regularly after the murder. Matt's death "motivated me to be out more in Laramie and try to educate people about what 'gay' is all about," he says. Mike joined a town diversity committee that has since ordered a Southern Poverty Law Center video on tolerance for use by Laramie public school teachers, and he has been deeply involved with the Unitarian church's efforts to become a "welcoming congregation": "They have a workshop curriculum that people can go through that really examines in depth all these different issues. For the most part the Unitarians are a pretty liberal group, and it's been mostly preaching to the choir. [But] what I've found is there are a lot of people who are open-minded, they believe that there shouldn't be discrimination, but they don't know any gay people, and they are afraid of them, of saying something inappropriate, thinking they need to be treated with kid gloves." Mike says he can relate to that anxiety:

> I grew up with no black people around, and I've had to come to terms with my racism. I think my classism is the bigger problem. Seeing someone on the street who looks like a homeless person, regardless of race, I have bigger issues with that. But I can translate those feelings. . . . I try to learn from those experiences. For years and years we've heard that you should not be racist because it's bad, or you shouldn't be homophobic . . . you should be ashamed. I really think that needs to be turned around: here is why it's cool to know African Americans, here is why it's cool to know gays. Diversity empowers you: knowing gay people helps you out, even if it's so that you don't feel that internal tension: "What would my friends say if they saw me talking to a gay man?" I was homophobic, I went through all of those fears, so I know what they're like. I see how freaked out people get sometimes when they contemplate going somewhere where there might be gay people. . . . That was actually a gratifying part of being involved with the Unitarians. I think a number of people were at that kid-glove stage. I feel good that my involvement with them has shown them . . . I'm just another guy, not fragile.

Mike's earnest activism has extended into charmingly odd locations. In the winter of 1999 he and several other LGBTA members spoke in front of the Rotary Club about gay life. "First you need to understand how a Rotary Club meeting works," Mike tells me.

> First you have lunch, and then they sing songs, have a raffle, and announcements from other clubs around the world. And then all the people who have to get back to the office get up and leave, and then you have the panel discussions. One of the Unitarians is a Rotarian, and knew me, and scheduled the panel. [I thought] this is something I want to do—speak in front of some of the leaders of the community. I was nervous going into it, because I didn't know how many people I would recognize (turns out not very many). And the other thing was that after doing their business meeting the people who didn't want to be there got up and left, and left a large audience of people that wanted to be there. So big

sigh of relief. They asked very good questions, were very attentive, came up and thanked us afterward, shook our hands. That was a really positive experience.

When we speak in the early months of 2000, Mike tells me that he was really pleased at the turnout at the vigils and Gay Awareness Week events right after the murder.

> But life goes on, and the interest and the emotion has faded away, and it's really quiet now. . . . It's amazing how quiet the place is. But at the same time, it has triggered ongoing thought. This community will never be the same. Everyone's got a full life, and you've only got a small amount of time, and the best we can hope for is to raise awareness, and that some people will have a little extra energy to devote to these issues. We're all pretty busy surviving, and I get frustrated sometimes about how slow things are moving. But still it's good.

In Val Pexton's opinion, "the truth is that folks in Wyoming really are deliberately out of the loop" about the gay men and lesbians among them "and try to keep it that way. Not because they're idiots, and not because they're rednecks, but just because they've gotten away with it, and they're trying to stay in that comfortable zone." Chad and Larz echo Val's belief. Like many of the gay residents I've spoken to, both Chad and Larz trenchantly defend Wyoming against its harsher critics, even as they acknowledge the difficulties of gay life in Wyoming. Chad tells me, "Not all people in Wyoming are completely bigoted. That's not true, at all." He resented the fact that after the murder many people outside the state considered Wyoming "completely redneck" because that perception "erased a lot of people I know, the university, a lot of people in Wyoming. . . . Wyoming is not as narrow-minded and not as redneck as it has been painted. At all. It's a very beautiful state. There are a lot of very beautiful people here." Chad—like many residents of the state, gay and straight alike—feels for Wyoming a love strung of affection, impatience, longing, and, most of all, contradiction: "As much as I don't want to live here . . . I grew up here. It will have a place in my heart." Likewise, Larz announces, "I am proof that you can be gay and open and happy and successful in Wyoming." Speaking in the familiar tones of insiderish and perverse Wyoming pride, he describes his descent from an old "pioneer" family who came to Wyoming "when it first opened up. While other people were going to California, we had to pick this barren desert in the middle of Wyoming." Larz himself tried that cross-country journey: "I lived on Castro Street in San Francisco. I worked out in an all-gay gym. Not only were all my friends gay, most of them were men. What a wonderful life, what an easy life." There was nothing wrong with that choice, he says, "but I think our family has some awful, recessive gene that forces us to choose a difficult life. The frontier gene—I've got the frontier gene. I've chosen to live in Wyoming. It's not easy to be gay here, it really isn't . . . but that frontier gene is active in Wyoming and dies in San Francisco."

At the HART Center, Peggy witnessed a new concern and seriousness about gay issues. She feels Matt's death had a positive effect on Wyoming, because so many talked about the murder, about anti-gay hatreds: "Wyoming has become an open place—we're more aware of it now, as a population," she believes. And Laramie and Wyoming have indeed held a long discussion about gay life and rights in the aftermath of Matt's murder—a halting, often reluctant, often ugly, and often heartening one—but it remains unclear what exactly that conversation has done to improve life here for gay and lesbian residents. That is not to say the individual support so many straight residents have articulated has been unwelcome. Ann, for example, is an employee of the university, a lesbian woman who felt enough at risk when she moved to Laramie to return to the closet after years out of it elsewhere ("Ann" is a pseudonym). Ann remembers the vigils before Matt died with real gratitude; although she was offended by the first vigil's defensive focus on the images of the university and state, still,

I was glad that so many people showed up at the Newman Center vigil. It made me feel like there really are people out there who
care. But it wasn't until way toward the end that a gay man who
grew up in Wyoming stood up and said, "Yeah, this is a gay issue."
Everyone else was saying it's not a gay issue, it's about hate, I don't
know what. I went from there to the Unitarian [vigil], and I spent
most of it crying, along with everyone else crying. The support
there—the first thing that Jeff Lockwood said was "welcome to
this safe place." And I just burst into tears.

After the vigil, she went to thank Lockwood, the president of the
church fellowship, and he said, she remembers, " 'It's not you who
should thank us but us who should thank you, for being open
with us and sharing who you are.' And I burst into tears again."
For Ann, who had spent the week of the attack feeling "isolated
and vulnerable," Lockwood's words were transformative. In the
university department where she worked, she had thought, "I
can't talk to people about this here. A major thing is going on in
my life, and I can't talk to most of the people around me about
it." Ann came out to many people that week but was glad she
didn't come out to everyone. A student told her that some members of her department thought Matt got what he deserved; such
news made the Unitarian vigil all the more moving.

And such moments do linger. Lisa, of the LGBTA, tells a funnier
version of Ann's story. She describes a conversation with a
coworker shortly after Matt's death: "It was a discussion about
ethics—we were doing the whole 'What do you think about
homosexuality?' discussion without actually saying that. She
started talking about her husband and how her husband really dis-
agrees with it and all those people should go to hell. But she said
that she really thinks that sucks, and she has friends that are gay,
and 'Shit, I don't care, they're just people, and we're all people
underneath.' And I was like, 'You are so fucking cool—I love you.'
" Stephanie chimes in: "Isn't it funny, that you find someone who
is willing to acknowledge you are not the Antichrist, and you're
like: 'You rock!' It takes so little to make us happy."

Chapter Three

Mary Jane's first reaction to the murder was swift and painful:

I'm so ashamed to be from Wyoming. I'm so ashamed to have to tell people that I live in this town. But very quickly that changed. Very quickly I felt exactly the opposite: I am so proud to be from this town. I didn't expect the kind of community coming together that I saw, the kind of support for the gay community that grew out of this. I didn't expect to see so many different kinds of people with tears in their eyes. People were so sad; students would come into my office and would be in tears, in my building people were in tears—people were sad, were so sad for what had happened to that young man. For myself it was like the death of a family member, and I saw that in people. It was that depth of feeling. And that carried on for a long time. It just generated a depth of feeling I've never seen before. I have to admit, here in the university community, we are sort of sheltered from whatever else might be out there. But I made a point: when I would go to the grocery store I would listen, and when I went to get my hair cut I would listen, and I was trying to see if there's another side to this community that I'm not hearing. And I'm sure there was, but I personally did not hear it. . . . I think that there's a genuine goodness in people here, and something like that happening here, something that sad—they're going to feel it because that's the kind of people who live here. I really would never have known that or thought that unless this had happened.

Bill Smith, a gay man who grew up in Laramie in the 1950s and 1960s and now lives in New York, feels a deep protectiveness toward Laramie: "This was a wonderful, wonderful town to grow up in. . . . When you talk about growing up here, it was this huge extended family." He fixes me with an intent look: "I don't ever want to say I'm not from Wyoming. I want people to identify Wyoming as me." Bill's words, and the words of Mary Jane and Ann, are a powerful corrective for those who would presume Laramie is the home only of gay death and straight hatreds. But it is true too that in Laramie straight support has rarely tread beyond the emotional register. Only occasionally, as Mary Jane among others has pointed out to me, has it been translated into

much of anything in the way of efforts to create meaningful public, political shifts in the landscape. (Jeff Lockwood, who has
helped to administer a memorial fund raised by the Unitarian
church for state organizations promoting tolerance and who has
led the local fight for bias crimes legislation, is a major exception.)
I would argue instead that if a single factor has improved gay and
lesbian life since Matt's death, it has been gays and lesbians themselves, people like Ann and Chad and Travis and Jim and Mike,
who have come further out since Matt's death, staked a stronger
claim to daily visibility and political action both. Clearly the outpouring of sadness and support from straight residents has made
coming out easier, but the widened openness of gays and lesbians—in the aftermath of such a brutal murder—was a brave
thing nonetheless. We'd be reminded of that, here in Laramie, in
the first spring after Matt's death, as the trial of Russell Henderson neared.

CHAPTER FOUR

On a chilled, foggy Monday morning—April 5th, 1999, a little past 7:30—I walked through the quiet heart of Laramie to the Albany County Courthouse, a broad-shouldered and boxy sandstone building flanked by the county detention center, an auto parts store, an apartment building, and a few local businesses. Jury selection for Russell Henderson's murder trial—the whittling down of five hundred prospective jurors—had mostly wrapped up here the week before. A last-minute court hearing had been called for later in the afternoon, postponing the final seating of the jury and the start of the trial itself until the next day. You'd think that would mean the courthouse would be calm, deserted this early in the morning, but it was anything but. Weeks earlier, Fred Phelps had announced his intention to picket the trial's first day, and the results of his announcement could be seen that morning spread across the courthouse lawn.

Phelps, a tall, gaunt figure in cowboy hat and red, white, and blue jacket, huddled with about a dozen family members inside a cramped, makeshift enclosure of black plastic fencing—the "Demonstration Area," a patch of brown grass backed up against the west side of the courthouse, prepared expressly for his arrival. Several of Phelps's fellow protesters were children—most appeared to be under ten. Like their elders, they clutched signs: "God Hates Fags," "AIDS Cures Fags," "UW Fags," "No Special Laws for Fags," "Fags Die God Laughs." One child hoisted a sign depicting two stick-figure silhouettes engaged, presumably, in anal sex; the text read "Fag Sin." Phelps himself displayed two boards: the one in his right hand, a giant photograph of Matt Shepard, read, "Matt in Hell." (A full year later, Phelps's Web site still included a page depicting Matt's face jostled by animated flames.)

But it was hard to see Phelps and his band. Ringing the fenced demonstration area were a dozen angels, their enormous, seven-foot-high wings spread wide, deliberately blocking any clear view of Phelps. The angels—heads wreathed in halos, white-sheeted wings draped over PVC pipe frames—were counterprotesters: several students from the LGBTA (Jim Osborn among them) and a few Denver activists. Their backs turned to Phelps, the angels remained silent; they'd decided in advance to avoid the shouting matches Phelps usually inspires. The "angel action" was not an original notion—it's an old anti-Phelps maneuver the protesters picked up over the activist grapevine. But it was a striking one nonetheless, a witty repossession of the sacred by the very people Phelps deems profane and damned. The angels, focused and solemn, felt the morning's cold weather. I handed my coffee over to one and later watched as Renné and another LGBTA member stepped from angel to angel, offering whispers of support and a box of tissues.

The cops were in attendance too. Several, drinking coffee and talking quietly, stood near the protesters, and a few were stationed on the courthouse roof, ready for trouble. Rob DeBree, the murder's lead investigator, was tucked in his courthouse basement office preparing for the trial; not wanting to give Phelps the honor of an audience, he still snuck a peek at the angels, delighted at their short-circuiting of the protest. A few yards from the angels, the Reverend Lou Sheldon, founder and chairman of the Family Values Coalition, stood, suited and soundbite-ready, in the courthouse parking lot. The coalition, according to its Web site, desires a "restoration of the values needed to maintain strong, unified families"; chief among its targets is "homosexual advocacy" (bias crimes legislation also comes under heavy fire on the site as a presumed form of pro-homosexual indoctrination). That morning Sheldon told reporters that homosexuality is a sin, but gays—like alcoholics and criminals—can be saved. The reverend was lovingly tended by a publicist, who told me that Sheldon had come to demonstrate that not all Christians were like Phelps (if only, as in Sheldon's case, in the more slick masking of their anti-gay politics). When he discovered I was from Laramie, the handler inched his pin-striped torso a bit closer to me and confided that a trial would be preferable to a plea bargain for Henderson, because "we trust the people of Wyoming to handle this situation correctly." Nearby, two representatives from GLAAD and the Gay, Lesbian and Straight Education Network (GLSEN) handed out press releases and smiled their encouragement to the angels. A handful of Laramie residents wandered by during the hourlong protest to check things out. But the real audience—certainly the only sizable audience—was the media. The previous fall Laramie had watched as its broadcast twin had grown and slipped free, taking on its own narrowed but persistent life; the media attention had eased through the winter, but now, with the first trial beginning, the attention had returned with redoubled intensity.

Bev Secklinger, a video artist, professor in Arizona, and former Laramie resident, had shown up, grabbing footage for her indie documentary about Laramie since the murder, but otherwise the media in attendance were all TV and print types. And there were a lot of them: they outnumbered all the protesters, Phelps and foes both, by almost two to one. The journalists, camera operators, on-air talent, and sound recorders formed and re-formed in small groups like schools of fish, engaging in desultory chat, answering cell phones, smoking cigarettes, honing sign-off lines. One or two occasionally split off to check messages or warm up in the "media village," a collection of trailers and tents set up by the city a few yards away. Just beyond it, satellite trucks packed the public parking lot, waiting to transmit. But despite the media readiness, there was little in the way of eye-catching action to record—it was a remarkably quiet scene. When Phelps and a young bearded man in a knit cap snarled out a brief, rather incoherent exchange, they were immediately surrounded by cameras and mikes; the only other times I heard Phelps get into his anti-gay groove were when reporters approached him to ask for a statement.

As I studied the oddest of Phelps's signs—"Save the Gerbils," almost quaint in its folkloric homophobia—I began to realize why the morning felt strange. For the LGBTA members who rose that morning before dawn to prepare, this confrontation did indeed feel like a pressing battle on turf they want to call home. But otherwise little of this seemed to be happening in Laramie. The town, and the people who live here, were bypassed by this scene. We'd provided the opportunity perhaps, but the opportunities were all for people from elsewhere—national activists, anti-gay Kansans, Sheldon and his publicist, journalists from local affiliates, from the networks, from Court TV, from the WB. They were all here to talk to each other. In part we were bypassed because the angels stayed purposefully silent, and in part we were bypassed because very few of us had come, having been urged by the town mayor and President Dubois to ignore Phelps's baiting. But mainly we were bypassed because the story could be made without us. Whenever the gathered reporters noticed what looked like an interview happening, they rushed to capture exactly the same one. You could watch the story being born, watch the characters chosen, watch the plot narrow, grow transparent, with each mirroring of effort, each concentrated, winnowing repetition.

I remember approaching Romaine Patterson, a pretty, young lesbian woman from Denver, who along with Jim Osborn had masterminded the angel action. Patterson, a former Wyoming resident, had befriended Matt during the year before his death, and fiercely mourned his passing. A few minutes earlier, aglow with energy, she had whispered a press release explaining the angel protest to the attending media. I wanted to thank her for her work with the LGBTA—Patterson was the person primarily responsible for providing the angels' impressive wings. As we started to talk, several cameramen sidled up, lassoing us in a tight loop of microphones and lenses. I remember watching her focus blur and then shift, as—still looking in my direction, still talking but no longer to me—she began to repeat her press release and announce that she'd be available to the media later that day to answer their questions. The morning was like that. It made sense, of course, the seizing of media opportunities as a deliberate corollary to such deeply symbolic activism. The opportunities had after all been created by Phelps's protest itself, his eager promotion online, his chats with reporters; Romaine, that morning's angelic public relations officer, was merely, and necessarily, responding in kind. Phelps's protest style strikes me as fairly cartoonish, but going up against the rawness of his anger is still no walk in the park, and the young gay and lesbian protesters who took him on that day were a moving and stalwart bunch. But that morning also struck me as symptomatic of the real Laramie's disappearance from the radar and the enthronement of another Laramie in its place. There was a true showdown on that courthouse lawn between Phelps and the counterprotesters outraged by his presence, but at the same time that stretch of grass seemed like some talk-show green room, aflutter with promotional materials and scripts, packed with handlers and newsmakers, an antechamber to minor celebrity. When I introduced myself to Cathy Renna, the GLAAD representative in attendance—despite my cranky cynicism about the media presence, I was hoping to interest her in making some grassroots connections with the LGBTA—she handed me a press packet. In a low voice of thrilled intensity, she told me she might have to leave the protest for a while, to run off more copies.

Six months later, on the first anniversary of Matt's death, Renna would tell me that she found Judy Shepard "so much more genuine" than most of the Hollywood celebrities she usually dealt with in her job. We were standing in the kitchen of the UW president's home, Mrs. Shepard a few feet away, at a party thrown in honor of Peter, Paul, and Mary, who had just given a concert memorializing Matt, at the president's invitation and the university's expense. (They weren't the first well-traveled singers to appear in Laramie: earlier that summer, in June, Elton John had come to town to perform a benefit concert in Matt's memory.) The party mingled an unprecedented mix, for Laramie anyway: lugubrious sixties' sentimentality, embodied by Peter (Mary, suffering from altitude sickness, had retreated to her hotel room, and Paul, tired as well, had also skipped); university grandees fingering jumbo shrimp; and young lesbian members of the LGBTA, clustered protectively together, a few dressed in defiant drag. As I got a drink at the bar, I noticed a party arrangement on the counter: a card, emblazoned with the PPM song title "If I Had a Hammer," leaning faux-casually next to an actual hammer. In that faintly surreal context, Renna's comment, its seamless blending of the real and the fake, grief and celebrity, Shepard and stardom, made a kind of sense, managed to get at the strange way America seems to understand authenticity these days: that TV cameras, or the presence of celebrities, aren't necessarily falsifying or merely exploitative; that instead they might somehow give confirmation, even richer life, to a loss. That the broadcast, be it TV, radio, or Web, the brush with the machinery of celebrity, makes an event real for its participants, not just for its observers.

The Gay and Lesbian Alliance Against Defamation, consecrated to monitoring and improving media representations of gays and lesbians, does its work in that glinting and treacherous territory of celebrity culture, and while it's easy to make light of press packets and Hollywood gossip, Renna and GLAAD take popcultural ephemera seriously, understanding that the constant recycling of glib and demeaning imagery takes its toll, however indirectly, in the attitudes and self-understandings of those who consume it. Renna helped the Shepard family navigate the complexities of the media that year, and she also worked the press during the court proceedings, vigilant for creeping incursions of homophobic sentiment. To Jim Osborn, warmly nurtured by Renna during the media deluge after the murder, "GLAAD walks on water." Clearly, GLAAD's cultural savvy, its sophisticated interventions in media imagery were welcome in the midst of a crime that inevitably called up ugly clichés: that Matt must have been trolling for "rough trade," or that gay men get what they deserve. But GLAAD's interest in the national dimensions of gay death was never matched by much of an interest in local Wyoming gay life. As with many other national gay and lesbian organizations that denounced the murder and even invoked it in their fund-raising, Wyoming itself was mostly a place to pass through on the way to the press conference.

Jim Osborn, as much as he defended GLAAD when we talk, had harsher words for the Human Rights Campaign. "I was very disappointed by them." Before Matt's death, in the winter of 1998, Jim, as a representative of the LGBTA, had attended an HRC banquet in Denver. "At the time I guess I looked at myself as a podunk kid; they brought me in for this dinner where the meals are one hundred fifty dollars a plate and everyone's running around in tuxedos, and here they are schmoozing over me. I was starstruck." But in the months after Matt's death, the shine wore off. Jim notes that the HRC has fund-raised heavily using Matt's image but that otherwise Laramie lies on the margins of their interest: "Their spokespeople spoke in Fort Collins and Denver, but they never came to Laramie—except when the executive director came for the Elton John concert, and that was because Elton was donating part of the proceeds to the HRC. I think they used Matt as a political tool, and that bothers me. He was not a person to them. He was something they could use one month before the elections." It's important to note that Judy Shepard has worked closely with the HRC's campaign for the inclusion of sexual orientation in federal bias crimes legislation—the organization clearly has the family's cooperation. Still, the HRC's lack of interest in local Wyoming issues has rankled. John Little is less blunt than Jim, but, he told me on the phone early in 2000, the UGLW "definitely noticed the national fund-raising. 'Resent' is too strong a word, but we definitely noticed it. The money was going out of state, and it caused some hard feelings here or there, in discussions over coffee and cigarettes. Elton John and all this came in, and did we see a dime? Hell no. Does anybody out there know that we exist?"

Little quickly concedes that a few organizations did know: the field organizer of the National Gay and Lesbian Task Force, for example, has provided welcome "technical support," offering strategies for "growing" the UGLW. The NGLTF also contacted Jim Osborn in the first days after the murder, and Kevin Jennings of GLSEN waived his honorarium to speak on campus a year after Matt's death. But, Little argues, "The most important thing we needed at the time and could still use is financial support." The Laramie Unitarians awarded the UGLW a small grant out of funds they had raised after the murder, but otherwise, Little says, "no money came back." Likewise, I haven't been able to unearth donations, beyond the Unitarian fund, to any other local LGBT-supportive groups.* While a few members of the LGBTA have been flown to national vigils and conferences, the group as a whole has received no donations from national organizations; neither did it get anything out of the Elton John concert, which raised funds for the HRC, GLSEN, the Southern Poverty Law Center, the Simon Wiesenthal Center, the Matthew Shepard Foundation, the Northwest Coalition for Human Dignity, and a University of Wyoming professorship in civil liberties. Indeed, a few months after John's appearance, the university actually asked the LGBTA for $2000 (nearly half its budget) to help pay for the Peter, Paul, and Mary concert, as the singers, happy to lend their name to the memorial events, nevertheless charged a $42,500 appearance fee. (In the end, the university lost $20,000 on the event.) I don't doubt the authenticity of the outrage expressed by national gay and lesbian organizations, activists, and celebrities at Matt's murder, but it seems to me that such postures of outrage and denunciation carry with them an ethical obligation to the lives that persist here.

Of all the out-of-towners who passed through Wyoming in the months after Matt's death, Elton John was easily the most popular and perhaps the most aware of those obligations. His June 1st con-

---

* In the spring of 2000, the U.S. Diana Fund (a charity named for Princess Diana) awarded a $20,000 grant to provide general diversity training and bias crime prevention on Wyoming's Wind River Indian Reservation. The UGLW participated in the application for the grant and will help to administer the new programs created by the award.

cert sold out and raised $250,000 in charitable contributions. John, who had dedicated the song "Don't Let the Sun Go Down on Me" to Matt at several performances that winter, had decided himself to come to Laramie and hold a fund-raiser, and while most of that money went to out-of-state foundations, some of it would trickle back to Wyoming through the Northwest Coalition, which includes the state in its grassroots agitation against a variety of big-otries.* During his concert at the university Arena-Auditorium (usually the site of college basketball games), John expressed his grief and told the enthusiastic crowd, "When I fly over America on my broomstick, as I often do a lot, I get to feeling what a big country this is. It's big enough for everyone. This concert is about ending hate." While a few audience members told local papers that they thought John's words would have a positive effect on local intolerance, others I spoke to were less sanguine about the political effects of concertgoing. Travis told me he saw the concert as, at best, a symbolic gesture that gave straight residents of Laramie a temporary chance to feel good about themselves. When a friend told Travis that this might be his only chance to hear Elton John—concerts of such magnitude being a rare event in Wyoming—Travis thought in response, "Well, I hope so," because what had brought John here in the first place was something he'd rather not see repeated. Mary Jane Trout enjoyed the concert but still felt it let some folks slide off the political hook: "I saw the governor come in and sit down. And then a little bit later Matthew Shepard's parents came in, and they sat right by the governor and his wife. And I thought, you know, you sorry son of a bitch, how can you sit there by the parents of that murdered son, and listen to the comments that Elton John has made, and think about all that's happened, and not have supported a bias crimes bill in this session?"

* As I concluded this book in the spring of 2000, the Matthew Shepard Foundation, organized by Matt's family, had not yet formally announced its system for dispensing funds, and the uw Law School professorship in civil liberties (to be named after Matt) was years, and many thousands of dollars, away from formation. Presumably, both will have an eventual, salutary impact on local gay and lesbian politics.

Numerous gay residents told me the same thing: the concert was a lovely thought, but the money could have been better spent elsewhere, creating lasting, public space for gay life in Laramie and Wyoming. Renné, for example, wistfully imagined the community center $250,000 could buy. And gay men and lesbians weren't alone in such longings. Carina Evans told me, about both the Elton John and the Peter, Paul, and Mary concerts,

> I think the university thinks that is the right way to remember Matt. But I think [there is] no real talk about what happened, what can we do to make sure it doesn't happen again. It's important to remember, but maybe the act of remembering is enough. We don't need these big events to tell the rest of the world, yes, Laramie, Wyoming, is remembering Matt Shepard, [that] we're embracing diversity now, we're bringing in Elton John. Well, yeah, it's good that he's here, just for the fact that it brings in a musical event and something to do, but people were looking to him to make some kind of statement about tolerance. Why do we need him to make that statement when we can make that statement ourselves? But nobody wants to do that.

When I ask her what the statement could be, she talks about making institutional rather than merely symbolic changes: beefing up diversity requirements in the university curriculum, setting up a gay and lesbian studies program. And when I ask Mary Jane the same question, she imagines creating an LGBT office on campus and extending full benefits to same-sex partners. "Those are the ways we should remember Matt," she says.

Bill Dobbs of Queer Watch, another out-of-towner, felt a similar dissatisfaction with the concert's political anorexia. Earlier in May, he began hectoring John and his publicist, pushing John to use the concert as an opportunity to advocate for antidiscrimination legislation: "If Mr. John lived in Wyoming, he could be fired from a job, evicted from housing, and refused medical care—shocking but true—because there is no Wyoming law to stop discrimination on the basis of sexual orientation." He also pressed John to oppose the death penalty in the trials of Henderson and McKinney. He had little effect: John's publicist told the Casper

Chapter Four

Star-Tribune that John had "a long-standing policy of avoiding political statements." But what was striking to me, in all of this, was how completely so many of us had assumed that concerts and cultural entertainments were the proper setting, even the engine, for political change; that celebrities could, and indeed should, translate their fame, and our lovestruck identification with them, into political authority. I have no problem with taking the battle for gay rights into any terrain, stardusted or otherwise. But, as one student put it to me, clapping for Elton John one week wasn't going to make it any safer for gay men and lesbians the next. And it seemed to me, as I listened to straight professors tell me how moved they had been by the concert, how important it was, that a purchased ticket and a few shed tears didn't count much as political action; and that it was a dearly bought mistake to let oneself think otherwise.

I've continued to wonder over the extravagance of emotion Matt's death has inspired, both here in Laramie but also nationwide, among all sorts of strangers, gay and straight alike. The media attention to the murder, its broadcast intensities, its bedecking in celebrity outrage, seemed to pull the distant within reach, make the stranger intimate and available. A letter writer from New York told the campus paper, "I don't think I've ever felt so at a loss for words. I'm horrified and angry. I'm saddened and exhausted." Another letter, from California, announced, "Never in my life have I been so affected by a stranger." A third, dramatic missive began: "How my routine has been rocked again this week. . . . Reading through every word in each article and each letter about Matt leaves me drained and crying. . . . I just cannot comprehend the emotions storming my body and soul as I write." Memorial Web sites and tribute pages sprang up across the Internet; one, written in the form of a letter to Matt, eagerly listed the celebrities who had denounced the murder and cried, "Suddenly, though most of us have never met you, we have all came [*sic*] to know about you, and your impact is still thundering in our hearts." The letter went on to compare Matt to Princess Diana.

In the October of Matt's death, the Casper *Star-Tribune* published a short essay by a twelfth grader who knew Matt as a child:

"I remember once, when I was in the second grade, Matthew played the lead in one of our elementary school's plays. About a week later he accompanied his little brother, who was on my soccer team, to a soccer potluck. Standing near me he was a giant, the first celebrity I'd ever met." The writer recalled his second brush with Matt, a year later at a Boy Scout meeting. Matt and his fellow scouts stood on a stage, recipients of an award, "but the adults had neglected to tell them to return to their seats. As a guest speaker prattled on, the boys stood at attention. Moments later young Matthew fainted. His knees were locked, and he fell flat on his chin. After receiving seven or eight stitches, he was again my celebrity." Something about this small story echoes the writing Matt would inspire among strangers as well—the charisma of vulnerability, the pull of theater. That Matt—whose youthful and attractive visage appeared frequently in anti-hate ads on MTV in 1999—had become something of a celebrity was unsurprising but still fascinating. He was invoked by presidential candidates and television actresses, eulogized by rock stars, compared to dead princesses. What could possibly link a brutal murder in a remote landscape to such things? Perhaps such linking is merely characteristic of a national political style that proceeds, all too often, through the mechanisms of iconhood and adoring identification, through the expression of emotion as itself a political good. Movements do need their martyrs, and emotion can indeed be the glue that binds citizens to action. But what happens when emotion is the only action in town?

The other, meager forms of help that did arrive in Wyoming, in the year after the murder, often arrived in rather arrogant fashion. John Little tells me,

> UGLW did make some very good contacts with some national organizations; we have received some good knowledge and support from them; but we've also realized that we can't let them over-

run us either. They tend to do things like they do in Washington, and that doesn't fly here. We had been talking with one [group] about doing some work around community organizing for antiviolence-type groups and working toward bias crimes legislation, and while talking to them and coming up with a plan of action, their people came up with this big, huge plan that we'd be recruiting hundreds of people and forming antiviolence projects in five or six different locations around the state. Well, you'd be kind of lucky to be able to talk to twenty or thirty people to begin with, in the entire state. The experience we've had is there tends to be in any community maybe a handful, if that, of people willing to do anything at all.

The out-of-state organizers typically reacted to such news with incomprehension; while rural communities are clearly becoming more important in the struggle for gay rights, the encounters I've heard of between veteran urban activists and rural gay men and lesbians are still halting, fraught with a complex mixture of goodwill, impatience, and condescension.

What remains striking to me is how few gay and lesbian residents of the state, beyond Jim, John, and a handful of others, even knew of the attempts at contact by outside organizations and activists. Somehow, despite the intensity of attention the murder drew, gay men and lesbians who live in Wyoming still felt marooned. Renné perhaps put it the most plainly to me: "I hoped for a little more help," especially, she says, with the bias crimes debates that absorbed Wyoming in the winter of 1999. She waited for national organizations to arrive, but as far as she could discover, "nobody showed up to talk, to explain. This is what these guys do, but nobody came to do that. It was really sad to me. We could have used the help, we could have used the local help," not just the lobbying in Washington, D.C. "They do great things, but they could have helped us more. They were preaching to the choir—they were talking to the people who already know and already understand. It's like going to San Francisco and saying we need tolerance." The national organizations, she says forcefully, should have come to say "why this would help Wyoming too."

Bypassed, as Wyoming so often had been, still the winter of 1999 did not end in absolute quiet. On Saturday, March 27th, in the midst of jury selection, a few hundred residents of Wyoming gathered in Cheyenne for Equality Begins at Home, a march and rally dedicated to gay rights (part of a nationwide effort organized by the National Gay and Lesbian Task Force and the Federation of LGBT Statewide Political Organizations). This being Wyoming, the marchers encountered thunder, rain, hail, and sun on their half-mile walk. Later that afternoon, safely ensconced in a hotel, a range of speakers—including Wyoming religious leaders, state senators Jayne Mockler and Keith Goodenough, NGLTF leader Urvashi Vaid, and the UGLW's John Little—exhorted the audience to support gay equality and urged the assembled to fight for another round of state bias crimes legislation in the next year. Nine days after the rally, Phelps arrived in Laramie.

Back on that April Monday, Phelps moved his protest from the courthouse to the university union a few blocks away. Again, he was greeted by plastic fencing (red this time); again, police lingered on nearby rooftops; again, angels surrounded him; and, again, a few individuals engaged him in debate, although with little in the way of explosive result. This time, however, most of the media stayed at the courthouse, awaiting the results of the impromptu court hearing. Instead, a good number of staff and students milled about in the sun, and the angels now found it hard to resist the occasional wave or chat with passing friends. A mere block from the protest, a DJ began to spin records: Parties not Prejudice, a light-hearted rebuttal of Phelps's grim intonements, was under way, sponsored by the LGBTA, undergraduate multicultural groups, the social work student organization, and—in a gesture of perhaps unlikely but still welcome solidarity—the UW Cycling Club. Clearly the DJ had put some thought into his playlist: as the Village People rolled out of the speakers, I watched two angels silently dip their wings back and forth to the beat. Phelps packed up early. After he left, the angels stripped off their wings and, joined by other members of the LGBTA, scrubbed the ground where he had stood, a symbolic gesture I'd heard of from past tales of the Lesbian Avengers. By late afternoon, it was as if Phelps had never been there.

Any lingering interest in his spectacle had by then already been supplanted by the results of that day's court hearing. Henderson, facing the death penalty for his participation in Matt's murder, had decided on the eve of the trial to plead guilty. Henderson and McKinney both had claimed since their arrests that Henderson's participation in the murder had extended solely to driving the truck and tying Matt to the fence; McKinney, they said, was the only one to wield the gun that night. Still, because of his participation Henderson was charged with both premeditated first-degree murder and felony murder and after watching the jury selection, watching citizen after citizen agree that, yes, they could consider the death penalty, Henderson and his lawyer must have realized that execution was more than a theoretical possibility (indeed, Henderson's attorney, Wyatt Skaggs of the public defenders office, acknowledged to reporters that his goal had always been first and foremost to save his client's life).

I spoke to several Laramie residents who were among those considered for the jury (I myself was part of the initial jury pool in McKinney's trial). For each of them, the death penalty issues covered intently by the twenty-page jury questionnaire and voir dire process provoked some hard introspection about an issue none of them had considered all that deeply before. Jan, a lively and handsome woman who works at Wyoming Public Radio, told me she began to read voraciously about the death penalty after being tapped for the jury pool; she eventually developed a firm stance against it. Another prospective juror reached a similar conclusion, publishing these thoughts in a letter to the Laramie *Boomerang*: "Two weeks of reflection [during jury selection] have made me realize that, no matter how grievous the crime, I can no longer condone the taking of a life for a life. . . . I hope we learn to promote the sacredness of life, so that no one chooses to kill another human being or stand idly by and watch while someone's rights are being violated."

The debate rippled out beyond jury selection, into the town

itself. The Laramie Ministerial Association, a group composed of numerous local religious leaders, announced its opposition to the death penalty in the weeks before Henderson's plea, as did the Wyoming Church Coalition. "Revenge," Chesle Lee, chair of the coalition, told reporters, "is not Christian behavior." The St. Paul's Newman Center, Father Schmit's university Catholic parish, which had organized the candlelight vigil months before, took out a March 25th ad in the *Boomerang* critiquing the death penalty as both a failed deterrent and a practice counter to church teachings; the center offered itself as a "place of refuge" for those who wished to pray and talk during the difficult weeks ahead. Echoing the Church Coalition and the Ministerial Association, the Newman Center urged Laramie to consider the value of forgiveness.

But there was less talk of forgiveness among the gay and lesbian residents of Laramie I knew. While the lesbian and gay community was just as split as the rest of the town over questions of life and death, punishment and justice, the anger so many had felt over Matt's murder had barely begun to fade. Ann, for example, received a jury summons for the McKinney trial and found herself struggling with questions of punishment: "I had trouble answering those questions on the questionnaire." She remains ambivalent about the death penalty for Henderson and McKinney both. "There's a part of me that feels like, yeah, they should get the death penalty for doing something like that. And at the same time there's a part of me that doesn't really feel like that's going to do much good." Mary Jane felt less uncertainty: "I would have much rather that Henderson had gone to trial, to tell you the truth. I was disappointed when he did not have to go to trial, because at that point there was a good chance he would have got the death penalty and I think he deserves to die. I think he deserves to die. I want them [both] to be judged by their peers. I want them to get the harshest punishment possible." She paused for a moment, thinking the question through. In a voice edged with anger, she added something I'd heard more than once: "Maybe life is the harshest punishment. Because he's a pretty young man, and he's going to be there a long time. So maybe that is the harshest punishment."

Lisa, never one to pull conversational punches, told me something similar. Lisa had studied criminal justice in college and knows some details of the Wyoming prison system: "I take great, sadistic pleasure in knowing that once they get to prison, once they go to Rawlins, they go through an introduction process that the other inmates call the fishbowl, or the fishtank. The new inmates are called fish. Once they get indoctrinated, then they're released into the population. Those guys are going to be bent over and take it up the ass until they're killed. The inmates are going to kill them. Because what they did is so low, and they're punks— punks don't last long in prison." Renné had thought too about the punishments, official and underground, Henderson and McKinney might meet. "That's really a challenge to me," she said. "I hate the idea of the death penalty." Yet, as someone planning a career in law enforcement, Renné feels she has to support it. "But I think it's a cop-out; it's more expensive, and what do we get out of it? These two guys are small guys, and men's prisons aren't known for their hospitality. Being a small male in a large-man prison, they're going to get their due. They're going to spend the rest of their lives in there, and to take them away from that early—that's a cop-out to me. I'd rather have them live, in that prison, having what they dreaded the most happen every single day of their lives." I've sometimes felt uneasy around such arguments, understanding their emotional force but also wondering if they brush up against something akin to homophobia: that the worst punishment imaginable is not death but forced sex with men. Renné has felt that unease as well: "I know that's horrible, and it's so mean, but the thought of them worrying every day of their life in there. . . . That's worse for me, so [it is] much better" as a punishment. "It's a horrible thing, but there couldn't be two more deserving individuals in the world than them."

Bill Dobbs told me that the vengefulness that undergirds such sentiments—and that underlies the death penalty as well—troubles him deeply, because such arguments skip the rails, abandoning the greater goal of justice in favor of emotionally satisfying punishment. In views like his, as heinous as the crime was, it is not an excuse to endorse other crimes, crimes of torture or death against the perpetrators. Cal Rerucha, the county prosecutor in charge of the case, pondered the question of justice as well, the day of Henderson's plea bargain. At the press conference after the plea hearing, Rerucha told reporters, "I think justice—you see it on the entrances to law schools, but it's very difficult to talk about what justice is. There are two people—Mr. and Mrs. Dennis Shepard—and they will go home without a son." But Rerucha felt satisfied that Henderson had been sentenced by Second District judge Jeffrey Donnell to two consecutive, rather than concurrent, life sentences: "It is my hope," he said, "that Russell Henderson will die in prison."

Rerucha had come under some fire during jury selection for his opening comments to prospective jurors. Asking them if they could apply the law equally, he reminded jurors that Matt "was a victim that was different, a victim that was not the same as you and I." That comment was widely reported (I saw it in the *New York Times* coverage of the case), perhaps because it fed some coastal presumption that out here in the sticks homophobia would have wide latitude in the courts. If *New York Times* readers drew such conclusions, they would be wrong. Clearly, Rerucha's comment reflected some real awkwardness surrounding the question of Matt's sexuality, but the bulk of his address to jurors seemed designed to put them on notice that, no matter their personal beliefs, they were to treat Matt as their equal. And Rerucha had worked tirelessly preparing for the trials (defense attorneys for Henderson and McKinney filed well over two hundred motions, not to mention the dozens prepared by the prosecutor himself). Rob DeBree—who during the year after the murder took a total of five days off and typically showed up at the county courthouse around four or five each morning—told me that Rerucha put in just as much time on the case. And, interestingly, in the preparations for the Henderson trial both the prosecution and the defense played down the issue of homosexuality—it seemed an issue both sides found risky to address. The jury questionnaire, packed with inquiries about the respondent's stance on drugs, alcohol, and punishment, made no mention of homosexuality; and Skaggs, like Rerucha, was at pains to tell prospective jurors that the case was "not about lifestyles."

Chapter Four

That said, clearly the question of Laramie's "image" hovered over the proceedings. One of the many motions filed by Skaggs demanded that the prosecution not tell jurors that "society will laugh at them if the defendant is not punished adequately." Playing to Laramie's widespread frustration with the press, Skaggs told prospective jurors not to give in to the media's depiction of Laramie as a place guilty of anti-gay hate. Quoted in the *Boomerang*, Skaggs said, "Begin by disregarding the guilt thing, that we have to punish somebody to prove to the nation that we are not some dusty old cow town." (As Henderson's attorney, Skaggs clearly felt the intense pressure of that media attention—one day in March as he dashed through the courthouse parking lot, he pulled a white bucket over his head, presumably to get a moment of privacy as he ran the media gauntlet.) Still, the question of Matt's sexuality and the role of anti-gay hatred was muted in the Henderson proceedings (though they would return much more insistently in the trial of Aaron McKinney). Instead, the hearing on Henderson's plea bargain was given over to something else: the difficult accounting of what had been lost that night by the fence.

Henderson himself had little to say. Taking the stand without much expression, he recounted his actions the night of the murder. In his version, McKinney was the continual ringleader, he the mostly mute follower, driving the truck when and where McKinney told him to drive, tying Matt when McKinney told him to do so. Henderson claimed that in the midst of the beating he told McKinney to stop; McKinney, he stated, struck him with the gun in response, and he then retreated to the truck and stayed there until McKinney was finished with Matt. Rob DeBree told me that Henderson recanted that claim in a postsentencing interview; he never told McKinney to cut it out, Rob says, and while McKinney did indeed hit Henderson that night, it was much later, when McKinney, disoriented by the fight with Morales and Herrera, struck out at Henderson, thinking he was one of the other men. In Rob's view, Henderson's plea was deeply self-serving, and while Henderson did offer an apology to the Shepards and asked their forgiveness, his statement, judging from the court records, was adequate to the pro forma performance of presentencing remorse and little more.

Judy Shepard—who just two weeks earlier had appeared at an HRC-sponsored news conference urging Congress to adopt broader hate crimes statutes—was with her husband in the courtroom that day. The Shepards had moved, slowly but steadily, from their initial reticence about Matt's sexuality and life to a deepening willingness to discuss gay issues publicly and agitate for hate crimes legislation. In the months following Henderson's plea bargain, they spoke often at gay rights events and press conferences in favor of hate crimes legislation, sometimes joined by the family of James Byrd Jr., a black man dragged to death in Texas by whites in the summer of 1998. That afternoon in April, both parents addressed the court. People attending the hearing later said the depth of their grief was wrenching to witness. Both spoke directly to Henderson. Judy Shepard told him, "I hope you never experience another day or night without experiencing the terror, humiliation, the hopelessness and the helplessness that my son felt that night." But mainly they talked about Matt, offering a collection of simple reminiscences—the books he liked, the languages he spoke—that were perhaps the only way to calculate his absence, conjure the substance of his loss, and for that reason were all the more heartbreaking.

Also trying to gather up the story of a life that day was Henderson's grandmother, Lucy Thompson, who begged the court to sentence her grandson to two concurrent, rather than consecutive, life terms, so that Russell would not be taken "completely out of our lives forever." Lucy Thompson and her husband had raised Henderson for most of his childhood; she has babysat local children for years, and I haven't spoken to a single person who does not describe her in language of great respect and affection. Laced with aching sadness and regret, her statement to the court acknowledged that Henderson had had a difficult childhood, living mostly apart from his young and unprepared mother, a woman bedeviled by drinking; that he had caused great pain and suffering to the Shepards and the Laramie community both. But she asked too that the court see the Russell "we know and love," the child who had survived severe health problems as a premature infant, the young man working toward a GED. JoAnn Wypijewski reported in *Harper's Magazine* that between the ages of five and eight, when Russell lived with his mother, he witnessed and experienced plenty of physical and emotional abuse from the men in her life; Rob DeBree agrees that Henderson had some hard times at the hands of his mother's boyfriends. Even for those who knew Henderson, he'd become, by that spring, harder to see, a collection of facts, static, reputation, and rumor. A high school dropout—he missed a single paper, preventing his graduation—and an Eagle Scout; a beloved grandson and deprived son; a reputed user of meth who had watched the degradations worked on his mother by alcohol; a roofer with a drained wallet every month and vague dreams of escaping Laramie; a nice guy, an unhappy guy, a quiet but angry guy; a boy whose life began premature and sickly, like the life of the young man whose destruction one night in October he would abet and watch. If the answer to his capacity for such a night lay somewhere in Russell Henderson, it didn't rest in any single one of those facts, as much as people sorted through them for glimmers of explanation. If the answer could be said to lie anywhere, it lay buried deep in the mundane texture of his contradictory life, in the spiral of trouble, hope, and darkness that wound through his days.

For Lucy Thompson, the winter and spring of 1999 were painful beyond the devastated season of her grandson's punishment. Cindy Dixon—her daughter, Russell's mother—was found on January 3rd, frozen to death north of town, by a lonely strip of road slicing through Rogers Canyon. The death was initially reported as an accident, and even after the facts were in, Donna Minkowitz managed to claim in the *Nation* magazine that Dixon had staggered drunk out of a bar and fallen accidental prey to hypothermia. But while Dixon had indeed been last seen at a downtown bar and had been drinking that night, her body was found a good eight miles from Laramie, and her death, while caused by hypothermia, was not accidental. Dennis Menefee Jr., a Florida man, pled guilty to manslaughter the following summer.*

---

* His arrest and plea bargain were both announced before the *Nation* article appeared. Minkowitz's carelessness was particularly offensive because she had disparaged Laramie in the same essay for its "extraordinarily high" rates of violence against women and its supposed lack of a strong "feminist movement."

Rob DeBree investigated the crime, and he told me that as best as he can reconstruct, Dixon was picked up by Menefee some time that evening and abandoned or forced out of the car sometime later, far from town on a night when temperatures plummeted to thirty degrees below zero. There were signs, DeBree says, of sexual assault—police found her torn panties a few miles farther up the road from her body—but not enough conclusive evidence to charge Menefee with rape. But Menefee, already wanted in Laramie on a burglary warrant, was charged with first-degree felony murder in April and later that summer copped to the plea; he was sentenced to Rawlins State Penitentiary, the same prison where Henderson had been sent to serve his life term.

As the spring wore into summer, the legal story here would continue to unfold. Chasity Pasley, Henderson's girlfriend, had avoided a trial by pleading guilty, back in December, to accessory after the fact to first-degree murder. Her sentencing was delayed until after Henderson's plea, on the chance that she would be called to testify in the case of a trial. On May 21st, Judge Donnell sentenced a weeping Pasley to fifteen to twenty-four months in jail, minus credit for time served, and ordered her to pay $250 to the crime victim compensation fund. It was a harsh judgment; the presentencing investigation report recommended probation rather than jail time. Pasley told the court she had been unaware of the severity of the beating on the day after the attack, when she, Henderson, and Price ditched pieces of Henderson's clothing in a Cheyenne dumpster and her mother's storage shed (Henderson hid his bloody sneakers in the latter, Pasley testified, because they were new and he hoped to retrieve them). Pasley admitted she had lied to the police, initially offering a false alibi for her boyfriend. (She did eventually tell the truth, but only after Kristen Price had first broken down and told the investigators that Henderson and McKinney had been involved in the attack.) DeBree felt Pasley was truly remorseful, and indeed she apologized continuously the day of her plea hearing, talking about her work for the LGBTA, telling the court she'd lied only because she loved her boyfriend. But Rerucha, according to the *Boomerang*, told Pasley she had come to the courtroom "not for justice, but for pity," and Judge

Donnell, while acknowledging the sincerity of her regret, still felt her transgressions serious enough to deserve incarceration.

Kristen Price's trial on accessory charges had been scheduled to begin a few days later, on May 24th. She had been out on bond since December, caring for her and McKinney's baby, only a few months old at the time of the murder. In mid-May, the court announced her trial would be delayed, and months later, in November, after testifying in McKinney's trial, Price pled guilty to misdemeanor interference with a police officer. She received a 180-day sentence and served none: 120 days were suspended, and 60 days credited for time served. Like Pasley, Price acknowledged that she had lied to the police and disposed of evidence. While Price and Pasley had both eventually cooperated with police and displayed remorse, Price's sentence was much lighter than Pasley's, DeBree told me, because Price had been the first to recant the false alibis.

While the courts in April and May were mostly given over to the cases of Price, Pasley, and Henderson, the legal wrangling over McKinney's upcoming trial was also well under way. McKinney's attorneys, Dion Custis and Jason Tangeman, spent some time that spring weighing the possibility of changing venues for the trial, as the local jury pool could be considered tainted by the intense media coverage of the crime and its perpetrators. Laramie, however, with its liberal reputation, seemed a better bet than other parts of the state when it came to the death penalty. That was only one of many issues Custis and Tangeman raised in motion hearings that regularly grew heated. Much of the arguing was over facts, insinuations, and documents released to the press. Rerucha, for example, had filed a list of previous criminal activities McKinney had been involved in, as perpetrator, witness, or victim. (McKinney had a history of run-ins with the police and at the time of the murder was awaiting trial on charges that he had robbed a local Kentucky Fried Chicken of cash and a couple of desserts.) The media had reported some details of Rerucha's list, and McKinney's lawyers argued vociferously that the material was highly prejudicial, that Rerucha had filed it knowing the media would have access to it, and that it should be inadmissible at trial.

Rerucha defended himself, noting, according to the *Star-Tribune*, that he had attempted to limit press access at every step of the criminal proceedings.

Custis and Tangeman had also been wrestling with lawyers other than Rerucha. Shortly after Henderson's plea bargain, Custis had told reporters that Henderson's tale of McKinney's singular culpability was a fabrication, one that cast an unfair portion of the guilt on McKinney, who had yet to stand trial. Wyatt Skaggs retaliated on behalf of his client by publicly releasing letters attributed to McKinney. In one letter written to an inmate's wife, McKinney summed up his explanation of the murder: "Being a verry drunk homofobick I flipped out and began to pistol whip the fag with my gun." McKinney, to the disgust of Rob DeBree and other officers, had discovered in jail the dubious macho status of gay basher; that letter was only one of many instances, DeBree told me, in which McKinney bragged of killing "the fag," offering to sign autographs for other inmates. Apparently, once in jail anyway, masculine status mattered to McKinney. In another letter, written to Henderson, McKinney manfully offered to take the fall, urging him to "blame everything on me."

Frustrated by the release of the letters and fed up with the squabbling among the defense lawyers, Judge Barton Voigt issued a gag order to prevent all attorneys and public officials involved in the McKinney case from any further contact with the media. In his order Voigt wrote that the court's expectation of professional conduct, "as Mark Twain would say, has been flung down and danced upon." At the end of May, Judge Voigt also ruled to push back McKinney's trial. McKinney's defense team, facing a death penalty trial scheduled to begin in August and feeling unready, had requested the delay. They won the continuance, only to discover that the new trial date, set to best suit the complicated schedules of the court, the prosecutor, and the defense, would be October 12th, 1999: the first anniversary of Matt Shepard's murder. If anyone—the media, the nation, the many following the trial—had yearned for a story with shape and punctuation, a narrative come full circle, it seemed that we would get it in October.

Chapter Four

The story, that spring and summer, of Henderson's and Pasley's punishments was the story that interested the media. The satellite trucks and reporters surged into Laramie for a few days in April and May and then ebbed quickly away. For my part, however, I found that summer that what interested me more and more were the stories that happened in between the trials, in less photogenic venues, in less familiar genres than the courtroom drama. One story captured me in particular: that of Kathie Beasley, who at first glance might seem to have a few autobiographical details—self-described bouts with drug use, trouble in school, the potential economic stuntedness of Wyoming life—in common with Henderson and McKinney (she told me that she had smoked pot with Henderson, a nodding acquaintance, once or twice in the past). The comparison shatters fast under the weight of any belaboring, but Kathie has chosen the margins of Laramie too—albeit margins very different from the ones Henderson and McKinney chose—and the life I've watched her design here is as admirable as it is improvised.

That summer, Kathie was twenty years old. She is a bit over five feet tall with huge eyes under dark, slashing eyebrows, and she favors loose-fitting pants and old workshirts. Since I've known her, her short hair has been shaded at one time or another pretty much every color imaginable—my favorite, a bright, swimming-pool blue, appeared briefly early in 2000. When she laughs, she looks caught off guard by her own happiness. Kathie was born in Laramie; she says it took her full twenty years to like the town, but she likes it very much now. She is a skilled guide to Laramie's few underground scenes; she catches traveling punk bands at the Hickey House and the Mini (residences that double as occasional clubs), and when we stroll around downtown, skateboarders and young men with mohawks wave and call her name. Kathie dropped out of Laramie High School in the late 1990s; she tells me she was a poor student for a number of reasons, including the chaotic distractions of drugs and a tendency to skip great chunks of every semester. But what finally drove her out the door was the school's atmosphere after she and her girlfriend sought to introduce gay and lesbian materials into the curriculum.

Schools in Wyoming, like everywhere else in America, are profoundly fraught locations, where sex is simultaneously denied, repressed, policed, corralled, defanged for class discussion, and made tantalizing and risky again, despite the best efforts of adults, in the shorted-out circuits of adolescent discomfort and flirtation. Throw the frightened, thrilled, secret dawning of gay desire into that mix, and it's hard to imagine how anyone manages to just walk down a hallway and make it to class on time. Nicki Elder—an angel at the Phelps protest—was a student teacher at Laramie High in the 1999–2000 school year, and she can testify to the difficulty of saying anything definitive about the state of the school's sexual politics, especially since Matt's murder. "Things," she wrote to me in an email, "are both better and worse." She rolls off a list of teachers, mostly in English and psychology, who make multiculturalism the backbone of their classrooms, and she mentions a philosophy class at the school where discussions of gender and sexuality have struck her as open-minded and wide-ranging. But she also points out that sex ed classes at the school consisted mainly of lectures about abstinence—and homosexuality was a taboo subject. Students rallied after Matt's murder, signing pledges of nonviolence and respect, but in Nicki's creative writing class, students who wrote love poetry were deemed "faggots," and several students turned in short stories imagining violent downfalls for gay and minority characters. "Laramie," Nicki concluded, "is a complex community, and the high school is wrought with tensions that are all over our town."

Those tensions obviously aren't unique to Laramie. Mark Houser, a member of the Safe Schools for All training project, has worked in both Wyoming and Oregon to promote the safety of gay and lesbian youth in rural schools. A tall, slender man, Mark has gathered stories from around the state and knows that Wyoming schools have had their share of anti-gay violence. He mentioned to me one recent example from Jackson: a boy—heterosexual but mistaken for gay—who was duct-taped to a pole by a gang of kids. Mark also forwarded to me an email from a recent Jackson High graduate describing another incident. The author (who wished to remain anonymous) wrote:

> I was in my graphic design class and was finishing a project. A student exited the dark room and approached me for help with developing a picture. He entered ahead of me, and when I followed, I noticed there were four other students already inside. As I was developing the pictures, I heard one of them yell "FAGGOT!" and as I looked up, I was punched in the face. I left the dark room and reported the incident to the principal. We discussed what had happened, and then he asked me if I could "tone it down a bit to prevent further incidents." At the time I had long hair with pink stripes, a nose ring, and earrings. The students were suspended, and I went on with my life.

While those are fairly extreme cases, other teachers have described to me an atmosphere of often idle yet still pervasive anti-gay sentiment. Priscilla (a pseudonym), a lesbian woman and an elementary school teacher in Wyoming, told me that teachers as well as students sometimes contribute to that atmosphere. At the start of a recent school assembly she watched as another teacher broke up a whispering duo of girls: "You don't want to look like 'those kind' of girls, do you?" the teacher chided them.

Kathie herself didn't think she was anything but straight until her senior year: "One day, this girl asked me to go to the prom. I thought, sure, I'll go, I've got nothing to lose, I don't care." It would be fun, she thought, to cut through "all the red tape—fuck yeah, I'd go. Anyway, we ended up dating. And it was so strange, 'cause the whole time we were in high school dating each other I never thought I was a lesbian." Kathie and her girlfriend were the only two openly gay students at the school. It wasn't easy. "We would hold hands in the hallway, and people thought it was just a joke. But once people caught on . . . oh, she's a dyke, now they're queer . . . it started to get bad. To the point where people behind us were calling us fags, in front of teachers, it didn't matter." Kathie thinks that while faculty and administration did not rush to end the harassment, it was not necessarily because they were invariably homophobic; neither she nor her girlfriend was a particularly successful student—"I was the bad kid, she was the single mother"—and therefore, she acknowledges, both were already relatively marginalized within the school's radius of attention.

Kathie credits her girlfriend with the toughness to face the hostility head on. "We were like, this has to change. And she really got me into the [idea of] antihomophobia training and curriculum change." A school-endorsed event, AIDS Awareness Week was coming up; Kathie and her girlfriend, realizing that in the past the event had avoided grappling with homosexuality, considered requesting a gay speaker. "They had condom demonstrations, stuff like that, and I never really thought about how offensive it was that they didn't offer alternatives—'also, there's this whole other thing called gayness!' No one ever said anything." They moved quickly. "We made up some petitions: 'We believe that sexual orientation is a very valid form of identification and we want antihomophobic training or some kind of curriculum.' There were about ten other people who helped us distribute the petitions, and we got like three hundred signatures, about half the school." They also approached all the teachers at the high school; only two were willing to sign. Others, Kathie said, were supportive but afraid to put their names on the petition—they feared the consequences of endorsing such controversial requests. Kathie approached the principal with the signatures and asked for a meeting; according to Kathie, he was "floored" in response and did not pursue her request. Supported by the director of Fort Collins's gay and lesbian organization, Kathie and her girlfriend also contacted the school board. Kathie claims she was told that her suggestions were unnecessary, since Laramie High had no gay students. In the weeks that followed, Kathie's girlfriend abruptly moved with her family to Oregon. Kathie was alone. "It got to the point, I didn't know what to do." Juggling the still-new and confusing personal process of coming out with the deeply political commitments she had made at school, her sense of isolation and fear mounting, Kathie decided to drop out. She and her girlfriend never made it to the prom.

Since then, Kathie has worked at a local bakery and volunteered at SAFE, the domestic violence project in town. In the winter after Matt's death, she began steadily attending meetings of the LGBTA. I remember one of the planning meetings as the LGBTA readied itself for the arrival of Phelps in April; Kathie told the group she was inclined to be nowhere near the courthouse or the campus that day. She was thinking, she told me later that year, "I am so afraid of this guy, because he hates me. I had to ask a lot of questions that night—why would you want to do this, why wouldn't you just want to go home and cry? Because that's what I felt like doing that night. And I did go home and cry that night. But at that point, I was like, you're either going to be a lesbian or you're going to be in the closet. I've never been one to really hide, even if it means telling the whole world to fuck off. I really felt it was my obligation to myself to be out." Kathie tends to be a consistently relentless critic of what she considers her own failings. She ended up, a few weeks later, dressed as an angel, back turned defiantly to Phelps and his followers.

Kathie had felt frustrated with the LGBTA in the past, wishing it would tackle, with vigor and higher visibility, large activist projects rather than the social events it more typically chose to plan. In that context, the angel action felt thrilling. "I didn't sleep the whole night before that. I was up making this banner: 'What are you doing to stop hate?' " In the middle of the night, she slung the banner out her second-story window downtown. She remembers the next morning, as the angels gathered to prepare: "Romaine Patterson's energy was really great. Being there with all those people was really binding. And I wanted the media to be there. Everyone needed to see this."

Galvanized by that morning, Kathie continued to invest the LGBTA with her political energies. She planned a series of workshops devoted to the often-ignored issue of same-sex domestic violence. "I started these presentations and tried to get some money through the Unitarian church's Matthew Shepard fund, because it was costing me a lot." They didn't fund her, and it was a frustrating time for other reasons as well. While many members of the LGBTA expressed interest, few people attended, and the speakers Kathie invited often canceled. "It didn't happen, it didn't work out. So one day Amber Holen and I were meeting—she had always come to the presentations—and she said, 'I have this great idea.' " Amber was a university student at the time; she has a steady gaze, a sharp mind, and an arresting tribal tattoo on the nape of her neck. Her idea was an ambitious new organization: the Wyoming Anti-Violence Project.

Kathie loved it. She and Amber met often during the summer and fall of 1999 to create WAVP, brainstorming plans, writing bylaws, networking with Wyoming groups, and researching the issues and needs of their constituencies. "It seems so big," Kathie told me early that fall. "We're including transgender, bisexual, lesbian, gay, and HIV-positive persons" under the group's umbrella. When I asked her to describe her hopes for the project, she grinned. It's not merely a phone number and Web site she desires (although she confessed to a moment of glee when she pulled out her newly minted business card) but something with a grander and more indelible physical presence. "I want an office, preferably downtown, as a resource center, with a huge pride flag outside. And you can go in there and check out books about sexuality, being gay, being transgender, information about drugs for HIV; we want to have a couple of computers for Internet access, and videos, and a list of other organizations that can help you too. Just have a place where people can go and know it's okay."

That particular future may take some time to materialize; Kathie and Amber are still mapping the contours of the project, while holding down jobs and living full lives. But the effect of their plans is already being felt here in Laramie. In the winter of 2000, Kathie cowrote a grant with SAFE, creating a formal link to WAVP, and pushed Laramie's domestic violence advocates to take same-sex violence and LGBT issues more seriously than they had in the past. That same winter, Kathie briefly returned to Laramie High School, intending both to finish her degree and start a gay-straight alliance. But reentering a teenage world after a few years out of it was alien and frustrating; tough on herself as always and afraid of failure, Kathie nevertheless decided to leave. You could say that Kathie's activism often appears to be unfinished business, but to me there are no deadlines. She tests the ground, tests strategies, keeps moving. Everywhere she looks, she sees work to be done; she is sometimes quickened by that scope of need, sometimes daunted. Swinging wildly from determination to self-doubt, she sometimes holes up in her apartment for days. She yearns for an artful activism, not merely an organizational one, wishes that the glorious theater of the angel action could more frequently imbue the duller work of grant writing and address gathering. But in the Laramie after Matt's murder, Kathie sees the chance to pull the town's edges closer to its heart: "I've got a really good opportunity to get a foot in the door, and get things going here." Kathie, like WAVP and Laramie itself, is still a work in progress.

CHAPTER FIVE

Kathie—as well as Stephanie, Nicki Elder, Jim Osborn, and Romaine Patterson—would don their angel wings again in October 1999. Fred Phelps returned to Laramie, the number of his companions whittled to six, on Monday, October 11th, the first day of jury selection in McKinney's trial, National Coming Out Day, and the beginning of another Gay Awareness Week at the University of Wyoming. The week—flooded by the jeweled light and warmth of Indian summer—would feel like a concentrated recapitulation, an uncanny, plagiarized double, of the previous year: marches, vigils, memorials, court proceedings; Phelps, the media, all sorts of out-of-towners.

There were faint variations in detail: that Monday, five more angels than the original dozen stood on the courthouse lawn, and all of them were enclosed in a pen adjoining Phelps's plastic corral rather than freely ranged about him as they had been last April. (The city, concerned about possible clashes among the protesters, had asked that the angels accept a corral of their own.) But the general outline was the same, and the sensation of repetition intense, as Phelps, lugging the same signs, again moved his protest to campus, again trailed by the angelic band of counterprotesters. The media was back in force, with dozens of journalists milling about outside the courthouse in a rerun of the previous April. The night before, in the hours before the Peter, Paul, and Mary concert, the university had sponsored a candlelight memorial vigil on Prexy's Pasture. It too was uncannily familiar: the concentric rings of speakers, journalists, and listeners, the heartfelt words of the speakers (Dubois, Father Schmit, student leaders) falling into the media-saturated gap separating them from the two-hundred-strong audience. I stood on the grass with a guy named Phil, a wise, funny man in his thirties who was a longtime member of the LGBTA. At the vigil's halfway point, Phil shot me a look of exasperation, as reporters and cameramen—apparently surfeited with footage—packed up and jostled past us to the vans and satellite trucks parked thirty yards away.

The LGBTA and their supporters on campus had planned an enormous schedule of events that week—if gay visibility is its own political good, then the university was overflowing with activist riches that autumn. The Straight but Not Narrow table was once again positioned squarely in the student union's breezeway; panel discussions on gay life and anti-gay violence occupied union rooms usually devoted to the student senate. Prexy's Pasture was the setting for yet another memorial service on Tuesday, the anniversary of Matt's death; Kevin Jennings of GLSEN delivered the keynote address Wednesday night and screened *Out of the Past*, a documentary about gay and lesbian history. An LGBT-friendly band, Dear Marsha, arrived from Denver to perform a rousing concert Thursday night. The Front, a downtown gallery run by art students, invited Laramie residents to write down their thoughts about Matt and the murder and then hung the scraps of paper from strings; afloat in the air, they gently swayed as visitors walked through the gallery. Bev Seckinger, the Arizona video artist, visited the Front one night that week to show clips of her still-unfinished documentary *Laramie: In Love and Trouble*; she also treated the crowded room to a showing of her short film *Mommie Queerest*. That week, Bev and I checked out the UW theater department's skilled production of *Angels in America* (while the theater department said they hadn't chosen the play as a deliberate memorial to Matt, the director, Professor Harry Woods, wryly told the Casper *Star-Tribune*, "I'd be less than honest if I said that the subject matter wasn't timely for this university and this community"). Another artist, Adam Mastoon, brought *The Shared Heart* to campus, a collection of his photographs documenting LGBT youth, accompanied by a tolerance-teaching curriculum he had prepared with the help of educators. Adam, a warm and gentle man, had stayed a night at my house when he first arrived (occasionally that year I felt like a summit guide for the various out-of-towners scaling Laramie); he was moved, he told me, by the university's commitment that week to remembering Matt as best it could.*

The remembrances had begun the previous Saturday, when marchers had again walked silently behind a green and yellow banner in the homecoming parade. The copy didn't quite match the original: only fifty people participated, and the protest signs many had carried the previous year were absent. Without the signs, bystanders had some trouble understanding who we were—several shouted questions, wondering what in the world we were doing. We straggled along at the tail end of the parade, behind Wildfire, a university dance troupe riding atop a firetruck, blasting music and tossing candy to the parade watchers. Behind

---

* That week, on October 12th, Fort Collins hosted the premiere of *Journey to a Hate-Free Millennium*, a documentary made with the close cooperation of the Shepards. The film discusses the murders of Matt and James Byrd and also covers the shootings of thirteen students and teachers at Columbine High School. Several members of the LGBTA traveled to see the film, including Jim Osborn, who was interviewed by the filmmakers. Shown in various cities, it arrived in Denver in May 2000; it had not yet appeared in Laramie by that date, although the filmmakers assured the *Boomerang* that they hoped to bring it here at some point in the future.

us a streetsweeper rumbled along, scouring the road we had just traversed. Bev darted among the marchers with her camera, and newspaper photographers hovered a few yards to the side, awaiting the arrival of a photogenic moment. At the corner of Third and Grand, as we turned back toward campus, I ran into a few more out-of-towners: the Tectonic Theater Project.

Tectonic, a collection of New York actors and writers, had already visited town several times during the past year, gathering interviews for a play about the murder and its rippling impact on the people of Laramie. Like their director, Moises Kaufman, the group was a soulful, perceptive, and charismatic bunch. Leigh Fondakowski, the head writer, and Greg Pierotti, an actor, had been the first to arrive in Laramie, back in the previous November. "We got here just as most of the media was leaving, which was very opportune for us, because people still needed to talk, talk about how they were being misrepresented in the press," Leigh told me one day in Coal Creek. None of the group knew what to expect from Laramie, except for the changeable weather: "That was a big joke in the company: we were all really overdressed—we all had these big puffy coats." For Leigh and Greg, two of the three gay members of the company, "driving to Laramie was a really dramatic experience. When we got here, we didn't know where we were going. We pulled into the parking lot over near the university, and we were terrified. We really felt like we were in imminent danger. There was nothing rational about it. But I think that was the first time that what had happened really hit me." Leigh's fear didn't fade until her third visit to Laramie, nine or ten months later. "I went for a run, and it was the first time I went out, other than for something to eat or for an interview, by myself." She freely acknowledges the irrationality of her anxiety—"I'm much safer here than I am in Brooklyn, New York"— but the haunting of Laramie by Matt's death, and the sense of isolation and vulnerability she felt because of it, was hard for her to shake.

The play—an artful and beautifully acted interweaving of the thoughts and stories of dozens of townspeople—would open in the February of 2000 in Denver and later move to New York. But back on that corner in October, Moises, Leigh, and the troupe's actors—all of whom would collaborate in the writing of the play—were still trying to make sense of Laramie. Leigh said the process took a long time. (I could relate.) In October 1998 she had participated in the "political funeral" for Matt in Manhattan, an intense and wild night of protest and clashes with the police. "I had a sense, especially after that, of having ownership of the story as a lesbian. So coming here, I realized, over the course of the year, [that], of course, it's much more complicated than that. And putting a human face on all of the people that were affected by it— it surprised me how much more complicated it was. I really thought I had it in a little package when I first came here." She and the company found themselves in a delicate quandary, as they tried to balance a complicated depiction of Laramie, including the ambivalence and disgust many here expressed to them about homosexuality, with their growing affection for the town. When the play opened in Denver, many of the Laramie folk who went to see it (including myself) told Leigh the play was too nice by half. She mulled it over with me that day in Coal Creek: "The reason why we're very kind to Laramie is because we love the people who live here. Literally. We forged relationships, [so] we feel this incredible sense of responsibility. We were so worried about betraying anyone's trust." The play did indeed tread deeply private ground, revealing (with her permission) that Reggie Fluty had been exposed to the HIV virus when she had tended to Matt by the fence, her hands covered in his blood as she did so. Matt himself, according to friends and family, was most likely unaware that he was infected.* Fluty spent the next year on AZT and eventually tested negative; her story winds through the redemptive heart of the play's depiction of Laramie.

The Laramie Project was not the only theater being made during the month of McKinney's trial. As the trial drew to a close, an obscure organization came to town and staged, on the courthouse

---

* According to Melanie Thernstrom's essay in *Vanity Fair*, Matt had undergone regular HIV testing after being gang-raped during a trip to Morocco. The results of the tests had always been negative.

lawn, their vision of an appropriate, poetically just punishment for McKinney: being lashed to a buck-and-rail fence and clubbed to death. The organization was ShadowGov, the latest crew to cash in on the press opportunities surrounding the murder and to use Laramie as a blue screen for the projection of their political ends.

Doug McBurney, one of the participants, had no qualms admitting to me that the performance was both political theater and publicity stunt (apparently the latter was mostly ineffective, as only a few print outlets and one Denver TV affiliate ran material on ShadowGov's demonstration). Atop a small trailer, McBurney and a few associates had assembled their main prop, a close replica of the fence on the prairie, from wood-grained plastic poles. The performer playing McKinney, dotted with fake blood, slumped against the fence and then slid lifelessly onto his back when untied. Another performer brandished a fierce-looking club, also stained with presumably fake blood. According to *West Word*, a Denver weekly, McBurney announced to the assembled media, "We request that the government officials of the state of Wyoming administer a swift, public, and painful execution of Aaron McKinney. Citizens of Shadow Government stand ready to execute justice upon the murderer!" Unsurprisingly, Wyoming declined ShadowGov's offer.

After some amiable email exchanges, Doug—a Denver resident—and I had a long phone conversation one day in the winter after the trial. Doug is a "shadow judge," and Laramie is, he tells me, part of his "jurisdiction." ShadowGov—a Web site, a training program, an online store, and a far-right Christian organization—is preparing "to take over the reins of government" after America's current system, "vastly wicked and corrupt," inevitably collapses. (Doug was quick to assure me that his organization does not advocate the overthrow of America; it merely expects it to happen sometime rather soon.) ShadowGov trains men (and men only—about forty of them so far) to "shadow" the criminal justice system, observing cases and judging them according to "biblical standards of law." "We're not too happy about democracy," Doug tells me. "It's unbiblical." When I ask him what kind of America he wants to create, he waxes poetic: "I want an America where one murder shocks the nation. . . . I would like an America that declares immorality illegal. I would like an America like it existed prior to the Constitution."

Doug tells me that he was drawn to the Shepard murder in part because of the fence, "a really powerful symbol," and in part because Matt "became a saint to the homosexual community and to the dominant media," a canonization Doug hoped to repeal (ShadowGov would "recriminalize" homosexuality). The McKinney trial, ShadowGov felt, was an ideal location for the organization to publicize its return-to-biblical-roots style of jurisprudence. Under the Shadow Government, there would be only three forms of punishment, Doug tells me: restitution, corporal punishment, and death. Prisons—essentially inhumane, in Doug's eyes—would be unnecessary, as shadow judges would issue swift, unappealable verdicts and dole out immediate punishments.

Doug is friendly and astoundingly loquacious, enough so that even as he denounces gays (homosexuality is "a tragedy" and "a deathstyle") and savages feminism ("men are naturally predisposed to govern"), it's hard not to feel some fondness for the guy. ShadowGov's founder, Bob Enyart, has a sense of humor too. His answering machine message at ShadowGov goes like this: "For updated information on Bob's national tour and ShadowGov demonstrations, press one. For Bob's shadow government mailing address, press two. And if you're an anarchist, an evolutionist, a humanist, a communist, a socialist, a garden-variety sodomite, a democrat, or a transgendered freak of nature, press three." Enyart, who cut his teeth in the antiabortion outfit Operation Rescue, announced the formation of ShadowGov by spending $25,000 on O. J. Simpson memorabilia, which he promptly set ablaze before television cameras. How exactly that action might symbolize the restoration of biblical order is unclear, but it has a certain undeniable flair.

ShadowGov, of course, is not all fun and games. On their Web site that fall—alongside a vast dissertation about JonBenet Ramsey and order forms peddling pamphlets and videos—McBurney

ran an open letter to Dennis and Judy Shepard. Replete with biblical citations, the letter repeated its wished-for plans concerning
McKinney and urged the Shepards' active participation in his execution. "At this point," the letter read, "you might be shocked."
But, McBurney argued, "the true culture of hate lies in the tolerance of wickedness." McBurney told me he hoped the Shepards
had read his letter but that he hadn't heard from them. However,
ShadowGov's three Web sites, according to *WestWord*, were aver-
aging one hundred thousand hits a week that fall. Apparently
someone was getting the message.

Back up and running, as ShadowGov had hoped, the Laramie
green room fielded a stream of visiting activists as well that fall.
David Smith of the HRC, Jeff Montgomery of the Triangle Foundation, Cathy Renna, and Bill Dobbs attended the trial and
worked the press. On October 9th, two Denver-based antiviolence
activists embarked on a Hike for Hope; journeying by foot from
Fort Collins to Laramie, they arrived at the fence on the anniversary of the beating.* The two men were cofounders of the BEAR
(Bringing Equality and Respect) Project, an organization dedicated to raising awareness in public schools through the distribu-
tion of teddy bears symbolizing victims of hate. The hikers toted
bears representing James Byrd Jr. and victims of the Columbine
shooting, and when they reached their destination they placed
"Matthew," the "official hike bear" dressed in khaki shorts and hik-
ing boots, on the ground by the fence and took pictures (it may
well have been the peak moment in the long transformation of
Shepard into a desexualized, childlike innocent). Renna and

---

* Another, much more ambitious hike had been announced the previous
spring by the International Hate and Violence Education (IHAVE) Foundation,
based in Washington state. Numerous organizations, including the Southern
Poverty Law Center, PFLAG, GLAAD, the Northwest Coalition, and GLSEN said
they would join IHAVE in planning a three-month, twelve-hundred-mile journey from Seattle to Fort Collins; Randi Driscoll, a San Diego singer/songwriter
who had earlier recorded "What Matters," a tribute to Matt, would perform at
a concert closing the hike. The planning of the march collapsed under the
weight of its own ambition sometime in the summer of 1999; the Hike for
Hope was its far smaller substitute.

Montgomery had joined the hikers for the final portion of their journey; the Casper *Star-Tribune* ran a photo of them standing tearfully next to the fence, Renna gripping one of the project's bears to her chest. The traffic in symbols continued apace that fall, the absorption of Matt into a currency of emotionalism, gesture, and image. Don't get me wrong: the commingling, out by the fence, of political witnessing and photo op didn't seem at all cynical, and neither did the activist attendance at the trial. As Smith and Dobbs, Renna and Montgomery jostled for soundbite room, I was grateful for their insistence that the national story of the trial, and of Matt, be shaped by pro-gay perspectives. And I understood that the teddy bears were meant to humanize the victims of violence, pull Matt and Byrd close to the schoolchildren who would clutch the bears representing them. But such gestures slicked the story's rough edges for quick consumption, and the furry sentimentality of the Hike for Hope struck me as the weakest of charms against the dark, spiky truths of the violence it wished to end.

Those truths would be unavoidable at the trial of Aaron McKinney. Like the rest of that recycled autumn, reading about jury selection in the local papers was disorienting. As in April, Rerucha reminded prospective jurors that Matt was their equal in the eyes of the law; Dion Custis asked them if they resented the media attention to Laramie and whether they might feel the need to "unshame" the community through their verdict. Image continued to matter, or at least the lawyers worried that it did. Rerucha echoed Wyatt Skaggs's query the previous spring: "Does anybody feel they need to make a statement to the nation that Laramie is not a cow town?" According to the *Star-Tribune*, his question drew no response.

With jury selection completed, opening arguments got under way on October 25th. Judge Barton Voigt had refused to allow the attorneys to ask prospective jurors about their sexuality; in a brief filed in August, Rerucha had argued that "sexual orientation does not rise to the level of bias or prejudice and thus cannot serve" to disqualify a juror, and the judge had agreed. Potential jurors could be questioned "as to their attitudes and beliefs concerning homosexuality," the judge said in an October 8th letter to the attorneys, but not about their own sexual preference. That bit of legal back-and-forth obviously pointed to a key aspect of the case: the question of homosexuality. And Jason Tangeman cleared up any lingering doubts about its centrality on the first day of the trial. Telling the jury that McKinney had been forced when five to perform oral sex on a neighborhood bully, Tangeman argued, according to the *Boomerang*'s recounting of his remarks, that "sexually traumatic events in McKinney's life, coupled with the influence of methamphetamines and alcohol, triggered him to attack." In the course of his opening statement, Tangeman told the jury that as a teenager McKinney had "engaged in homosexual acts" with a cousin, and at twenty had been distraught after he accidentally entered a gay and lesbian church in Florida. Arguing that Matt must have been looking for a sexual encounter that night—why else would he have left with McKinney and Henderson, he asked?—the attorney claimed that "five minutes of emotional rage and chaos" ensued after Matt allegedly grabbed McKinney's crotch and licked his ear. The gay panic defense had come to Laramie.

Deplored by lesbian and gay activists, the gay panic defense—a recent development in the ever-intensifying romance of jurisprudence and therapeutic culture—theorized that an individual with latent homosexual urges would spring uncontrollably into violence if propositioned by someone of the same sex. While Custis told the *Star-Tribune* that he and Tangeman were not engaged in such a defense—the defense team had not "ever stated specifically a gay panic defense," he claimed—the activists observing the trial, as well as Judge Voigt, felt differently. Voigt said in court that the opening statements had caught him off guard—Custis and Tangeman had never mentioned this defense strategy in pretrial hearings. Voigt told the two attorneys that he might disallow that line of argument if they pursued it during the defense phase of the trial; in the meantime, the judge said he would ponder the question while Rerucha made his case to the jury.

Clearly the prosecutor's challenge was not to prove McKinney's involvement—as Rob DeBree said to me, this case was "no who-dunit." Still, Rerucha led the jury through the story of that night, playing McKinney's confession to the court and calling various deputies, Price, Pasley, Herrera, and DeBree to the stand. (Henderson, having already cut his deal and received his sentence, refused to testify.) While mapping out the events of the previous October, Rerucha also clearly intended to refute any attempts the defense would surely make to mitigate McKinney's role in the crime or the viciousness of it. (In a witness list filed some time before the trial, Rerucha even included a member of the Humane Society, who could testify to the fact that the murder "would be cruel and brutal and not tolerated in a civilized society if this sort of beating had occurred on a domesticated animal, i.e., a cat or dog.") Custis and Tangeman had argued in their opening that McKinney's panic was intensified by meth and alcohol, and Rerucha endeavored to dismantle that claim systematically. Price testified that as far as she could tell, McKinney wasn't speeding the night of the murder; Pasley seconded Price, as did Matt Galloway, the Fireside bartender who had served both Matt and his attackers. Galloway also told the jurors that McKinney wasn't drunk when he left the bar, and Price mentioned that McKinney often tidied up the house when high and usually seemed happier drunk than sober anyway. The notion that booze and drugs might have spun McKinney into a rage seemed unlikely in the face of such testimony, and the expert defense witness who later argued that the crime had all the hallmarks of meth violence struck one courtroom observer I spoke to as a relatively ineffective counter-point to the eyewitnesses. Rob DeBree too was unimpressed by the argument—he told me quite forcefully that the murder didn't look like any meth crime he knew.

In his confession to DeBree, McKinney had denied using meth the day of the murder, and while McKinney had been arrested too late for the police to confirm this through blood testing, DeBree felt certain that McKinney for once had told the truth. Obviously it's unsurprising that the lead investigator would disagree with the defense, but DeBree had some compelling reasons on his side. "There's no way" it was a meth crime, DeBree argued, still passionate about the issue when I met with him nearly six months after the trial had ended. No evidence of recent drug use was "found in the search of their residences. There was no evidence in the truck. From everything that we were able to investigate, the last time they would have done meth would have been up to two to three weeks previous to that night. What the defense attempted to do was a bluff." Meth crimes do have hallmarks. One, "overkill," certainly seemed to describe what happened to Matt, but no others so seamlessly fit that night: "A meth crime is going to be a quick attack," DeBree pointed out. "It's going to be a maniac attack. . . . No. This was a sustained event. And somebody that's going to be high on meth is not going to be targeting and zeroing in on a head, and deliver the blows that they did, the way they did," with such precision. "Consistently it was targeted, and even if you're drunk, you're going to have a tough time trying to keep your target. No. There's just absolutely no involvement with drugs."

The testimony by Rerucha's witnesses was often wrenching. Reggie Fluty moved "even the male jurors to tears," Rob DeBree said, when she recounted finding Matt, thinking he was a child, pleading with him to "hang on, baby boy." The jury saw blown-up photos of Matt's destroyed face and head; the coroner testified that Matt had been struck at least twenty times with the pistol ("a big old Dirty Harry gun," DeBree called it when he showed me a photograph, that weighed close to four pounds). An acquaintance who had observed the trial told me that when the defense took over on Friday, October 30th, it seemed impossible that they could even begin to push back against the terrible weight of evidence against their client. What they did instead was accumulate evidence against Matt.

The defense had little choice, I suppose. Facing overwhelming physical evidence, a confession, and the death penalty, they had to work with whatever was left. They chose to open their defense with the testimony of a UW student who said he had been approached by Matt at the Fireside the night of the beating. The student testified, according to the *Star-Tribune*, that Matt had asked to sit with him. He had agreed but "began to feel really uncomfortable. I didn't like the thoughts I was having about the motives for him sitting with me." That line sounded more like a self-indictment than anything else, and DeBree says such friendly actions were typical of Matt's style; earlier that night, Matt had approached two women at another local bar and asked to sit with them. But obviously Matt might have been engaging in some casual flirting as well. The student described Matt as "small . . . small in many ways": "He carried a mini Bic lighter and drank a Heineken—which is the smallest kind of beer you can drink." What he revealed about Matt's departure from his table was perhaps more pertinent. Henderson came up to them, leaned close to Matt, said "Hey, buddy," and then whispered something inaudible. The student said Matt got up to leave, tossed a "sexual innuendo" in his direction, and joined Henderson and McKinney at the bar. In its coverage of the testimony, the *Star-Tribune* reported that he had kept an eye on the three because "he wanted to figure out whether Henderson or McKinney was gay."

Whatever that testimony revealed about masculine anxiety— and it seemed to reveal plenty—it distressed many observers, who felt the defense team was blaming the victim. Judge Voigt, meanwhile, was still pondering the gay panic defense. In a hearing earlier that day, without the jury present, the judge had questioned Custis and Tangeman. The two attorneys had argued, according to the *Star-Tribune*, that McKinney's "emotional response to the homosexual advance" should be admitted because it went to the question of intent: McKinney had acted in the "heat of passion" and panic and thus was unable to form malicious intent to commit murder (their goal was not to get McKinney off but rather to get the charge against him dropped from first-degree murder to manslaughter). Voigt seemed unconvinced, and on the following Monday he rejected their arguments, deciding that homosexual panic was not recognized as a legal defense in Wyoming. In his decision, Voigt argued that the defense would have to demonstrate that any reasonable person put in McKinney's situation would react in the same way—an "objective test." Instead, the defense seemed to be arguing that McKinney's "own reaction to his own past," as the *Boomerang* put it, was evidence enough to toss out the element of malice. But, Voigt wrote in his decision, "if a defendant has a low tolerance for letting his wife stay late at the bar, killing her would just be manslaughter. That cannot be the law. Is it murder if a white supremacist kills a white man who jostles him in a crowd, but only manslaughter if he kills a black man who does the same?" If you act on your own prejudices, no matter their origin, those prejudices can't then be used to excuse or mitigate your intention, your malice, or any act you commit: that seemed to be Voigt's point. The judge thus informed Custis and Tangeman that while evidence of McKinney's sexually traumatic past might be allowed in the trial's sentencing phase, it was off limits during the trial itself.

Observers of the trial felt nevertheless that the gay panic defense continued to seep insidiously into the remainder of the trial. David Smith and Jeff Montgomery said as much to the press, and Cathy Connelly, who has a law degree to go with her sociology professorship, felt the same. While Custis and Tangeman could no longer argue that McKinney's traumatic childhood experiences had led him to snap, they nevertheless created a picture of Matt as a sexually aggressive gay man who often threatened other men with his advances. The university student's testimony had certainly implied that, and on Monday McKinney's team wrapped up its defense with another, similar tale. A man who had tended bar in Cody, Wyoming, in 1998 testified by phone that Matt had made a pass at him that summer. Matt had tugged on his shirt and asked him to go for a walk; the bartender responded by punching Matt twice, knocking him out. The bartender felt, the *Star-Tribune* reported, that he had experienced "a momentary loss of reason" but told the jury that he didn't regret striking Matt.

During their portion of the trial, Custis and Tangeman, looking to minimize the murder's horror wherever they could, also tried to prove through various witnesses that the severity of Matt's injuries would have prevented him from feeling pain or cold that night by the fence and that some of the bruising on his body might have been caused by hospital tests. They brought out the meth expert on Monday. Otherwise, deprived of the opportunity to flesh out McKinney's traumatized past, they had little more to present the jury. They wrapped up their defense on Monday afternoon.

The next morning, in closing arguments, the defense attorneys appeared to skate perilously close to their original plan of attack. The *Boomerang* quoted Custis: Shepard, he said, "was innocent, but he was also forward. He was forward and people reacted to that." The crime began because Shepard provoked McKinney, and "it continued because of chronic methamphetamine use. . . . He lost his emotions to such an extent he hit Matthew Shepard too many times." Custis had argued that the beating itself took only a few minutes at most, and in his closing Rerucha reminded the jurors how long a minute could feel, rapping his hand against a table while ticking off the seconds: "It's a long time" he said, "if you are descending a road to hell." Rerucha asked the jury to remember that Matt had begged for mercy that night. "If anyone was born to be a victim in this case, it was Matthew Shepard." He deserves, Rerucha told the jury, "your protection."

One day later, on Wednesday, November 3rd, the jury returned their verdict: McKinney was guilty of two counts of felony murder (murder during the commission of kidnapping and aggravated robbery). He was acquitted of first-degree murder—the jury had not been completely convinced that McKinney had intended, with premeditated malice, to kill Shepard. Nevertheless, McKinney still faced the death penalty on the felony murder counts.

The sentencing phase of the trial was scheduled to begin the next morning. Jeff Montgomery predicted to the *Star-Tribune* that the "denigration" of Matt's character would likely intensify as the defense team tried to save their client's life. The jurors, however, would be relieved of that heavy burden. On Thursday morning, the Shepards, the prosecution, and the defense worked out a deal. McKinney agreed to two consecutive life sentences, the same punishment visited upon Henderson. His plea bargain also carried two other stipulations: he would not appeal the verdict, and he would agree to a lifelong gag order about the murder. His lawyers also agreed not to discuss the case. Rerucha told the court that Judy Shepard had approached him and asked that McKinney be shown mercy; only then did he go forward with the plea bargain. While I read many letters and editorials that November praising the Shepards' pity and forgiveness, Bill Dobbs, the Wyoming ACLU, and the editors of the *Star-Tribune* found the circumstances of the plea bargain disturbing. All believed the parents played too determinant a role in the sentencing agreement, usurping the place of the jury and judge. Dobbs also told me that fall that he felt the agreement forced McKinney to surrender his First Amendment right to free speech, and the *Star-Tribune* made a similar argument in an editorial soon after the trial. The Shepards seemed bemused by these criticisms and told reporters that the contours of the deal had been proposed by McKinney's own attorneys. The family welcomed their proposals, Judy Shepard told the *Star-Tribune*, because it meant "we'll just never have to hear" from McKinney again.

At the sentencing hearing, Dennis Shepard read a long, angry, and heartbroken statement to the court. In it, he mourned the passing of his father, who had died three weeks after Matt, from the "stress and grief" of that October. He remembered Matt, Matt's love of people, his "hope for a better world, free of harassment and discrimination." He spoke of Matt's many friends in Switzerland, where Matt had finished high school when his father had taken a job in Saudi Arabia. He spoke of the intolerable loss, of the "odd moments when some little thing reminds me of him; when I walk by a refrigerator and see the pictures of him and his brother that we've always kept on the door; at special times of the year like the first day of classes at UW or opening day of sage chicken hunting." He also denounced the death penalty politicking that had surrounded the case: "I find it intolerable that the priests of the Catholic Church and the Newman Center would attempt to influence the jury, the prosecution, and the outcome of this trial . . . by their newspaper advertisements and by their presence in the courtroom. . . . This country was founded on separation of church and state. The Catholic Church has stepped over the line and has become a political group with its own agenda." If anything, he told McKinney, "the crass and unwarranted pressure put on by the religious community . . . hardens my resolve to see you die." Shepard assured the court that he, his wife, and Matt were, counter to media reports, indeed supporters of the death penalty. "I give you life in the memory of one who no longer lives," Shepard concluded. "May you have a long life, and may you thank Matthew every day for it."

McKinney, like Henderson before him, offered a brief statement of apology: "I really don't know what to say other than that I'm truly sorry to the entire Shepard family. Never will a day go by I won't be ashamed for what I have done. That's all." Rob DeBree later told the *Star-Tribune* that twenty minutes after the verdict McKinney was "back in jail, smiling, laughing, and watching himself on television." I found it difficult that fall to condemn Henderson and McKinney fully—as a college teacher, I'd like to believe no twenty-two-year-olds are beyond redemption. But when Rob told me that he doubted the existence of McKinney's self-proclaimed remorse, it was hard to completely ignore the evidence.

Often that autumn I had heard acquaintances and commentators float the theory that Laramie needed the catharsis of a trial (rather than a plea bargain), an idea that intrigued me but left me unconvinced. Maybe it was because I wasn't entirely sure what we'd be released from, what gripped us that should be loosened. Trials—the real ones, as opposed to those waged on TV and in fat Grisham novels—aren't much in the way of purification rituals. They're too messy, too full of halfhearted stabs at meaning, failed narratives, witnesses mired in unease, and lawyers who fail to seize the cinematic moment. What could a trial grant us? That, with the proper verdict, we'd be able to "move on," slip past Matt's death and what it forced us to see? Or maybe that we could know, finally and without question, the truth of that night?

Certainly, both before and after the trial, the residents of Laramie and Wyoming in general continued to mull over questions unanswered. Why did Matt leave with his killers? What drove McKinney and Henderson? What precise and deep energies propelled that night?

Long after the trial, I still read letters to the editor calling the murder a bar fight or a robbery gone bad; I still heard that Matt died because he was gay. I still came across folks who believed that Matt was trolling for sex that night, that Matt wanted to buy drugs, that McKinney and Henderson offered him a ride home, that Matt asked for one. I still heard the frustrated question: why would he ever leave the bar with those two as companions?

Larz asked exactly that. "From everything I know about Matt's murderers, they had warning signals stamped all over them. Matt is European-educated, son of a good, good family, University of Wyoming student. What is he doing hanging around a couple of high-school-drop-out, drug-addict robbers? Punks? You don't see me down at the Fireside, trying to pick up men like that." Matt, Larz thought, must have been "desperate for something"—affection, attention, something.

Chad wondered too. "That's one question I'd have to ask: Why did you leave with these guys?" Chad worried about "blaming the victim," but still he'd like to ask Matt, "Whatever prompted you to want to leave with them? . . . I feel bad for asking that and wondering that, but at the same time I don't understand why." Chad would never consider doing what Matt had done: "No way. It's completely unsafe, completely." But even as he said it, Chad seemed anxious, as if his certainty somehow threw Matt's character into question. Chad's unease about "blaming the victim" was not unique. That Matt was an innocent victim—of which there is no doubt—doesn't mean that we need see him as innocent of sex, of desire; but in the minds of many I spoke to that year, to think the latter seemed to taint the former.

Ann thinks Matt was "misled," maybe "inexperienced" in reading people, and Bill Smith agrees that Matt may have been confused by the signals. Bill remembers a recent visit back to Laramie, when he exchanged smiles with a man in a local restaurant. "In New York, that's cruising. [But] I don't know what's happening here—I don't know if he's 'being Laramie'"—engaging in the casual friendliness of the place—"or if he's cruising. So I can see somebody coming from a cosmopolitan kind of background" and making the same mistake. Bill had thought too about the question of why McKinney and Henderson did what they did. "There's something missing in those guys. . . . They felt left out." Bill believes that in Matt they saw "someone attackable, someone vulnerable. . . . They [were] allowed to abuse this category of person."

Many of the other people I spoke to during the season of the trials had continued to mull the question of class, of McKinney and Henderson's potential resentment of Matt, a clean-cut student wearing stylish leather shoes and drinking imported beer while they paid for the cheapest pitcher in the house with quarters and dimes. Bob Beck, despite his frustration with the reductive media vision of Laramie as a town divided, buys a downsized version of the economic argument—that McKinney and Henderson were broke and saw an opportunity. It was, he believes, "a situation, clearly, where you have a couple of hooligans who have burglarized places, who were short of bucks, short of money, and they see a guy, a real little guy, [and think], this is a guy we can roll. We can rob this guy." Beck, who followed the trial closely, is most compelled by this story of that night: "They're sitting there, and they don't have any money . . . and they see him, and maybe he's wearing nice shoes, maybe he's wearing a nice watch, he looks like he's tipping a guy. Somehow they meet him, get talking to him. And they all take off. And the two of them say, I tell you what we'll do—we'll get him in our car, we'll take him out somewhere, and we'll rob him, and we'll just leave him out there. And I really think that was always their intention, that was always what they were going to do. And it developed from there." Beck considers Henderson and McKinney "Beavis and Butthead" redux. "These guys, the one thing I've learned covering this case, they weren't geniuses. You don't get arrested an hour or so after [the police] find the victim if you've covered your tracks at all." Other than wanting cash, Beck sees little intentionality at work; he doubts they thought, "Oh, we'll show that class, or we'll commit a hate crime. It seems pretty difficult to [believe] that they would think like that. They just think, here's a little guy, he's rich, we'll rob him. . . . And that's why the shoes are gone—to make it more difficult for him to walk. That's the way someone like McKinney probably thinks."

Mark—the fetish catalog purveyor and clearly a man of savvy economic understanding—thought class envy might have played a role in the killing. Although he doesn't believe such jealousies exist much in Wyoming, Mark wonders if Matt "exemplified to them two things that were very unknown to them: the luxury of finances and sexual orientation, [both of] which I think they couldn't understand." But most of the people I spoke to still had a difficult time believing that class resentment had anything to do with the murder. Carina Evans, for example, told me she doesn't see Wyoming as particularly class-conscious, simply because not many people have all that much money and the ones that do tend not to flaunt it. The conventional accoutrements of status, she believes, don't count for all that much here.

Mary Jane Trout works with underprivileged students at the university and senses something similar. In her job, she regularly encounters students from backgrounds so rural they can "find it scary to just come visit someone in their office. . . . In the city, people have to become streetwise really quick, but in Wyoming, there aren't that many streets." That's not to say such students are "hicks," just that they "don't really think about class issues. I don't really get that impression from Wyoming students. I think it's because a lot of people in Wyoming are poor, so these kids have grown up, and they don't really see themselves as being any different from the majority of people they know. You don't have this big line between them." While she thinks there is, objectively, a wide spectrum in Wyoming from poor to rich, clearly most people reside in that spectrum's less flush regions. Thus she remarks of the notion that the killers were motivated by class hatred:

> I thought that was bullshit from the first time I heard it. I could be totally in the dark, because I have a lot less feel for how young people feel in this community who are not affiliated with the university. But I think it made a very good news story. And in one way I think it's okay to draw attention to the fact that in Wyoming we do have this gap between rich and poor, but I don't think it had anything to do with them beating Matthew to death. I would think that those young people would think the university is an elitist institution, but that's not why they beat him up.

Mike, with the same methodical thoughtfulness he brought to his encounters with Unitarians and Rotarians, imagined a complex interweaving of class and other motives in the crime.

> I was angry at the social situation that let that situation develop: the homophobia in society making gays an okay target. And I have a lot of sympathy for the two guys—the examples they had growing up, the rough times they had growing up. I have a lot of understanding of how they could have so much anger. So I can understand how all the circumstances added up, the fucked-up lives that led them to drugs and alcohol as an escape. I think that social injustice is one of the roots of this crime. I think it's a much, much bigger issue than just a gay bashing. And I would not be surprised if there was some internalized homophobia—if [McKinney] were questioning himself, and anger was the result.

Like Mike, Mark wondered about the possibility of "latency." But while their speculations might seem to brush close to thoughts of "gay panic," neither Mike nor Mark believed such possibilities, if true, meant McKinney was less culpable—it merely struck them as a potential explanation, not an excuse, for his rage.

Stephanie took the investigation into larger questions of gender: "I don't want to say that anybody who's a bigot is queer and denying it, because that's reductionist and untrue—although I do have my suspicions about Fred Phelps. But there seems to be a fear of crossing gender boundaries. I really think that the resentment felt by certain heterosexual men toward gay males is because gay males are perceived as occupying a feminine position in sex, but they're male—so they're 'selling out the guys,' and that freaks them out." K. C. Compton, the *Star-Tribune* editor who had wondered if the fear of being a "sissy" worked on McKinney and Henderson that night, also mused in the same column about the absolute terror of sexual violation among straight men. She had little patience with it: "Welcome to the world of women, where, statistics show us, you have about a bazillion percent greater reason to worry." If being hit on were just cause for murder, she wrote, "my past would be littered with bodies, as would that of just about every woman I know."

Val Pexton—recalling the killers' violent entanglement with Herrera and Morales on the same night—saw race, class, sexuality, and other tensions less easily identified at work.

> It wasn't just about them hating a gay guy. They hated anybody who wasn't them. And that's more serious than boiling it down to one simple thing. That's the problem, that they've been brought up to hate, and not just to hate one person but to hate anybody who's not them, and given the right set of circumstances, this is what they can do—they can kill and hurt. That's more than just saying these are two narrow-minded rednecks who hate gays. That's not all they are, and so that means that's not all we are. Any of the details that fall away, that people somehow think are less important than other ones, make it even harder to know how to deal with it. Because you're trying to make it just one thing, and it's not.

It seems to me, as Val said, that whatever "it" was—precisely—was lost to us the moment that dark stretch of time began to unravel: lost because the beginnings, at the Fireside bar, were so unremarkable as to go mostly unnoticed, lost because Henderson, McKinney, Price, and Pasley began rewriting their script, over and over, the moment they began to tell it, lost because McKinney discovered in jail the cheap swagger of gay-bashing braggadocio and rewrote his part again, lost because Matt is lost. It seems to me, then and now, that the questions we in Wyoming most wanted answered—Did this happen because Matt was gay? Can we know for sure Henderson and McKinney committed a hate crime?—we were asking in the wrong way. Bias—homophobia or any of its cousins—rarely plays out, I think, in perfect focus. Discriminatory violence is rarely fully plotted—even in its most grotesque manifestations, it is far more often a bleak and ugly blur of knee-jerk discomfort, semiconscious revulsion, false visions of vulnerability, opportunistic rationalization, and relieved retreats to familiarity and sameness. If we wanted Henderson and McKinney to supply a version of homophobic violence so symbolic, so planned, so measured and pure in its intent and execution that we could not deny its existence, they were poor candidates. What they did instead was show us homophobic violence as it more usually expresses itself: half-hatched, half-confused, complex and impure of motive, deeply cruel, and utterly stupid. Matt is no less the victim of something unbearable if we say that his killers acted from a poisonous blend of intention and unintention, greed, resentment, rage, and hate in concert with other less nameable energies, if we say that a deep thread running through the crime was hatred of gays, rather than saying it was the only thread, the entire fabric of those events. That makes it no less a crime of bias; it instead makes it precisely a crime of the kind of violent bias that permeates our daily worlds. This is perhaps more difficult to legislate or fix, but it is crucial to see.

The person in Laramie who perhaps can see those things most clearly is Rob DeBree, bound, almost too tightly to breathe, to that night, to Matt and his killers, from the moment the 911 call set his role in motion. Rob, I suppose, looks exactly like a Wyoming cop, a proudly professional, toughly built man who spends his time off fishing and hunting. Rob is a sergeant in the Sheriff's Office, and his cramped office is squirreled away in the basement of the Albany County Courthouse (when he ushers me in, he intones, "Welcome to my tomb"). At first glance, the decor would suit the assumptions of the laziest out-of-towner: the antlered head of a buck adorns one wall, and a well-seasoned saddle lies on the floor, tossed down casually next to the filing cabinets. But look around, and you'll see the more complicated truth about Rob. Carefully drawn charts and time lines hang on bulletin boards, detailing open cases, and the photographs of murder victims—including Matt and Daphne Sulk, the fifteen-year-old murdered in Laramie the year before Matt's death—face his desk. You can see in these things both Rob's meticulous investigative intelligence and the intense, abiding sympathy he feels for the victims of the murders it is his lot to understand.

For anyone still believing homophobia had nothing to do with that night, Rob has an answer: "There's no doubt in my mind that this was a planned thing because he was gay. Matt was what I would consider to be identifiable as gay in his outward appearance, and obviously he was a good target for these guys. They wouldn't consider him a threat—he's not going to be able to do anything to them." Rob is certain that the two approached Matt, not vice versa, and that they deliberately tricked him into believing they too were gay. According to Price's testimony in trial, McKinney and Henderson plotted the deception in the bar's bathroom. In a postsentencing interview—"a debriefing-type situation"—Henderson also acknowledged as much. "You take most of these types of confessions and their story, you kind of take it fifty-fifty," Rob says. But in this instance Henderson "went into great detail about how they pretended to be gay to lure [Matt] out, changed their voices [to] an effeminate voice, probably [did] some touching. There's absolutely no doubt in my mind that Matthew did anything to start this," he says, slamming the words "no doubt" down like a hammer. McKinney's claim in his confession and the trial that Matt had grabbed his genitals was, DeBree asserts, "a flat lie."

Indeed, at one point in his confession McKinney denied that Matt had flirted or come on to him in the bar, while acknowledging "that he kind of thought [Matt] might be" gay. More than once in our conversation, Rob seized on the moment in the confession in which McKinney claimed Matt had touched him. To Rob, McKinney's syntax appeared to catch him red-handed in the act of fabrication. Rob read the lines aloud: "Well, he put his hand on my leg . . . slid his hand, like, as if, he was going to grab my balls." In Rob's opinion, that "like, as if" betrays the rest of the sentence's claim to factual reportage; whether or not you agree, it's undeniable that throughout his confession McKinney radiates hostility toward gay men. Slurs slide off his tongue without a second thought: When Rob inquired how he had met Matt, McKinney replied, "The fag? The queer?" Asked what Matt looked like, McKinney responded succinctly: "Like a queer." It goes on from there.

Henderson, Rob notes, wasn't nearly as "prevalent with the words." (Kathie Beasley remembers, however, overhearing Hen-

derson's casual demeaning of gays—"fag, dyke"—in high school.)
Both, however—and especially McKinney—clearly thought they
knew their lines, had the gay-bashing script down cold: if Matt
came on to them, then didn't he deserve what he got? McKinney
tried valiantly to make that case during the confession, although
in my reading, it never looked very convincing. Earlyish in the
confession, McKinney told Rob that he beat Matt because "he
tried to throw himself all over me. I don't know if he was trying
to get away or what he was doing, but I just remember getting so
mad." And again: "He asked me once to stop, then he was just
like all over me, trying to hug me and stuff like that. And I just
took my gun, and I was, like, 'Get away from me.' " Listening to
the implausibility of these claims, Rob felt he had McKinney
dead to rights: he "knew [he] was just going to have to spend
some time with him," and he would squeeze the facts out.

Rob asked McKinney if he hated gays. McKinney: "I really
don't hate them, but when they start coming on to me and stuff
like that I get pretty aggravated." So how many have times have
you been approached? Rob asked. McKinney: "This was the first
time." Huh. McKinney, of course, would change his story about
that night, about Matt, so many times in the year between the
murder and his punishment that it's unlikely that anyone could
have kept track. Taking a break, apparently, from his jailhouse
posturing, McKinney called a Cheyenne radio station on June
23rd with yet another version (it was his only contact with the
press). Rob leafed through a transcript of the radio interview.
McKinney told the interviewer, "I had no idea that Matthew
Shepard was gay"—which, Rob points out, contradicts his confession. McKinney argued that he was truly remorseful and not
driven by hate: "I don't hate gay people, I've got a good friend
that's gay" (beside that line in the transcript, Rob had written in
a burst of irritation, "Yeah, right"). Later, when the interviewer
asked McKinney if he had been despondent since the murder, he
seemed to forget about the remorse he'd been feeling and
answered no.

Rob thinks robbery was certainly on McKinney and Henderson's minds that night but feels the details of the crime simply don't

fit a mere robbery. "If you're committing a robbery, tie him up and leave him alone." In the confession, McKinney had shrugged off questions of Matt's condition: "I wasn't positive he was dead, but I thought he was probably gonna die." Rob believes McKinney must have been more certain that Matt was fatally wounded. "Matt's obviously going to be able to say who did this to him. They were going to kill him. How could they not?" Parsing McKinney's grammar eventually has diminishing returns, and Rob is clearly protective of Matt (he tells me the defense strategy of blaming Matt for instigating the attack by making a pass "sickened" him). But Rob and the documents are convincing. Part of the night's plan was robbery, no doubt, but—at the very least—Matt looked like a target to McKinney and Henderson because he looked gay.

While Rob is certain about the element of anti-gay hate driving the crime, he can't answer the question of why Matt left with Henderson and McKinney that night. "I don't know." He describes to me the earlier scene at the Library Bar, when Matt introduced himself to the two women patrons and joined their table. "I think that Matt was just so personable in a lot of ways. I don't know, and there's no way we are going to know. I do know that he did not ask for a ride home. I do know that it wasn't for drugs. And if they were portraying themselves as gay, it might have been a situation where he wanted some company. I don't know." What matters to Rob is what happened fifteen blocks from the Fireside—"Matt was in fear, there's no doubt in my mind, at Fifteenth and Grand." DeBree is sure that Matt knew by then that he was in trouble. And about two miles further down Grand, "the attack began to take place": McKinney struck Matt, seated beside him in the truck, with the gun, "and then it proceeds out. Of course, McKinney in a lot of ways tries to cover this as being a robbery situation, and"—Rob laughs dryly—"it's common, in any homicide investigation we have, no matter what they confess, they're going to try to minimize it as best as possible. But the attack actually initiates somewhere in the area of Wal-Mart and continues for a sustained period of time. I can only imagine that [Matt's] terrified, that he's absolutely terrified. There's no way that he can get out."

In his confession, McKinney had said that Henderson stood by laughing and cheering during the beating by the fence. While DeBree can't be sure of that, he does say, "We are convinced—even though Henderson denies it—we are convinced that Henderson was holding [Matt] while some of the beating occurred, due to the blood spatter on his coat." Henderson and McKinney had "a weird loyalty to each other: Henderson would not say anything bad about McKinney, nor would McKinney say anything about Henderson." But, "personally," Rob comments, "from all the evidence that we've put together, I wouldn't be shocked that a couple of the blows would have been delivered" by Henderson. "But not by the gun. I think the gun was all by McKinney." What matters most to DeBree is this: "They spent some time torturing this kid."

The media had reported that during the beating McKinney had asked Matt to read the truck's license plate. When Matt was able to discern the numbers, McKinney resumed the pistol whipping. Rob thinks that version is possible but has an interpretation he considers more likely. "I think essentially what happened is Matt probably made a statement, 'Don't do this to me, I've got your license plate.' I think he's doing anything he can to get out of this situation. That to us makes a heck of a lot more sense." Some jurors apparently doubted Matt could have read the plate that night; Rob went out to the crime scene after dark and got down on the ground where Matt had been tied. "You could easily read the license plate. There's no doubt in my mind that's what Matt did in hopes of trying to get them to stop: 'Don't do this anymore, I've got your license plate,' etc." That Matt did read the license plate and beg for mercy was significant to Rob beyond the cruel poignancy of such facts. "Right there—right there—is premeditation. I think that's the hardest part for jurors to understand, that premeditation can happen within successive thoughts. Everybody is so used to TV that they think [premeditation is when] you plan this thing for a week or so and then go and do it. But right there, if there was any doubt about first degree—that was it." Even if you trust McKinney's own statement, Rob points out, "where he says, 'I asked him to read the license plate and he did, so I hit him more'—that's premeditation. So, either way."

To Rob, figuring out what motivated McKinney and Henderson isn't complicated: "They were vicious people." He can't abide the excuses, the laying of blame on drugs or childhood traumas.

> The media in a lot of ways just infuriates me. They give so much credence to these murderers and don't spend near the time on the victims and their lives. They'll talk about what could have caused this, what could have caused this? My question to them is, who cares? There are people that are just plain vicious, that have absolutely no remorse for anything. They're cold. I don't care what caused it. There's nothing you can do about it. You can always find an excuse, I guess, or attempt to. But sometimes it's just that this person is a vicious bastard, and they deserve to get what they're going to get. Why give these punks credence?

The years Henderson spent with his mother were hard, Rob acknowledges, but he weighs that against Russell's life with his grandparents, "a loving family." To Rob, "Russell Henderson made his decision." Aaron McKinney's mother died from a botched surgery when he was sixteen, but, Rob says, "he still had family. Yes, I feel sorry for him, because of his mother. Who wouldn't? But I'm sure that his mother taught him that it's not right to kill. I'm sure his mother taught him that you don't just randomly take somebody because they're gay and beat them to death. . . . Aaron McKinney is Aaron McKinney, and he's where he belongs."

That day in his office, Rob walked me through his time line of the investigation. Less than forty-eight hours after finding Matt, the police would have all the evidence they needed, the result of a combination of good fortune and absolute relentlessness. On Tuesday night, Matt went first to the Library Bar, then to the LGBTA meeting, and then to the Village Inn. A member of the LGBTA drove him home, and sometime later he headed out to the Fireside alone. Meanwhile, McKinney and Henderson had knocked off work and dropped by McKinney's house to scrounge together some money; they too hit the Library Bar (after Matt's visit) and eventually made their way to the Fireside, at roughly ten o'clock. They probably first approached Matt as he sat at the bar, but no one knows for certain. No one knows exactly when they left, either, but it was certainly well before 12:43, when the Laramie Police Department received a call reporting a possible "vandalism in progress" in the vicinity of Seventh and Harney. The call was most likely about Morales and Herrera, who admitted they were out "doing crimes," as Rob put it, slashing a few tires. McKinney and Henderson were in the same spot for a combination of reasons. "Earlier in the evening, McKinney and Henderson had been attempting to sell this gun"; apparently their possible buyer lived in that neighborhood. "They went to the general area in the hopes of locating this guy again, but also in the same breath, they were also going to burglarize Matthew's house"—located nearby— "because they had tortured that out of him, as to where he kept his money and things to that effect." Down around Seventh and Harney, they encountered Herrera and Morales.

It's not entirely clear how or why the fight started. McKinney claimed Morales and Herrera "jumped him for no reason," but Herrera testified that the four of them saw each other and started talking trash. In Rob's view, Herrera's version is closer to the truth: "Some bravado statements were made between [them], and then McKinney, being the punk that he is, decided to go around back and hit Morales in the head. There's no doubt in our minds that if it wasn't for Herrera," who struck McKinney in the head with a stick he had handy, "there would have been another homicide."

When the responding officer arrived on the scene, he saw McKinney and Henderson sitting in their parked truck; Morales and Herrera had fled. When the officer flashed his lights, they jumped out, tossed something in the pickup bed, and broke in opposite directions. He chased down the driver—Henderson— tackled him to the ground, and then arrested him for interference. He ran the registration on the truck, discovering it belonged to McKinney's father. The officer noticed Henderson's wounded lip and took him to Ivinson Memorial Hospital. He had also seen the bloody gun in the bed of the pickup. When he told Henderson that he better not discover someone had been shot that night, Henderson reportedly laughed and said in reply, "You won't find anybody with a bullet hole in them." (The gun was unloaded during the attack on Matt, and Rob said police searches turned up zero ammunition in the truck and in McKinney's apartment.) After seeing a doctor, Henderson was cited, released from custody, and picked up by Chasity and Kristen. Apparently Henderson told his girlfriend something about the attack there at the hospital; Chasity told DeBree she argued furiously with him outside.

Between one and one thirty that morning McKinney arrived home, covered in blood both from the attack on Matt and from his own head wound. Washing the blood from himself and Matt's wallet, he told Kristen what had happened, or one version anyway: that "some queer dude" had hit on him in a bar and that he and Henderson had decided to lure him into the truck in order to rob him. McKinney told her to hide the wallet, and she obliged, tucking it in a used diaper. When McKinney told her his victim might be dead, she didn't believe him—her boyfriend, she testified, had a tendency to exaggerate.

Around two or two thirty that same morning, Morales arrived at Ivinson for treatment; friends had called his father, saying he was badly hurt, and his father had rushed him to the hospital. In court Rerucha would say that the dozens of stitches Morales received looked like a "bad sleeping-bag zipper." The injury was serious enough that Morales was transported to Poudre Valley Hospital in Fort Collins. The next morning, Wednesday, Rob visited the crime scene at Seventh and Harney. Peering into the truck from the outside, "you could see the card on the dash belonging to Shepard," he said. At the time, unaware of Matt's condition, the cops speculated the credit card might have been the spoils of a burglary, but McKinney was hiding out, so they couldn't know for certain. Rob said the truck was extremely bloody, but the fight the night before might have explained that. Rob also noticed one black leather shoe in the vehicle, something he "filed in the back of his mind." He filed away as well a memory of the truck's hitch, covered in dirt and grass—it struck him as strange, and he would remember it later. At around five that evening, McKinney arrived at Ivinson, head aching from Herrera's blow. At the same time, an officer was heading for McKinney's house, seeking information about the melee and the truck on Harney. Then, at 6:22, the 911 call about Matt came in—Aaron Kreifels had sprinted to a nearby house and begged the inhabitants to phone for help. Reggie Fluty, when she arrived on the scene, saw Matt's campus ID lying on the ground, and the case began to break as soon as it had begun.

Rob spent some time at the crime scene delegating tasks and then went to Ivinson Memorial to try to speak to Matt and take photographs of his injuries. Fluty accompanied him (in the future, she would return to the fence and lie down in imitation of Matt's position when she found him, so a police artist could make sketches depicting the scene). They pulled into the hospital parking lot and saw the same truck that had been parked at Seventh and Harney earlier that day. "I'd already been at the crime scene and looked at the tire impressions that were present; I immediately walked up and immediately saw that that was going to be the truck—there was no doubt in my mind," Rob recalls. The hitch was making sense now too: "Out at the crime scene, you could see where the truck had turned around and backed into an embankment—thus the grass and the dirt in the hitch. So obviously we were going to seize all that. And another big, key thing—now we knew who the black shoes belonged to, because Matt didn't have his shoes on at the scene. And the credit card was still there," in the truck, with his name on it—the same name that was on the ID card found out by the fence.

Matt, unconscious, obviously couldn't speak to DeBree, but Rob did talk with McKinney at around 8:45 that night. "Of course, he denied any knowledge of anything." When Rob asked him about the truck, McKinney offered the ludicrous alibi he and the others had cooked up in the intervening hours: a stranger had taken his truck the night before, McKinney told Rob. He claimed that when he and Henderson were at the Library, having a beer, he had left his keys on the bar for a while, and someone just up and took his truck. Whoever it was, he came back an hour or so later and invited McKinney and Henderson to a party on Harney Street. That's why they were there, McKinney explained—just looking for a party. To Rob, the fake alibi was "probably one of the most lame attempts I've ever [heard]. I told him straight up, I said, 'You're lying to me, McKinney.' I said, 'We'll be back together.' "

"He was a major suspect at that time, and I knew he wasn't going to go anywhere except Poudre. We contacted the authorities down in Fort Collins, as well as the security people at Poudre, and made sure they were going to keep an eye on him until I could put more of this together." Rob also asked Kristen some questions at the hospital: "Of course, she denied everything." The truck had been seized as evidence that evening, so Kristen called Chasity and Henderson for a ride home. They drove to Cheyenne to dump Henderson's clothes, which were covered, Chasity testified, in blood and bits of flesh. At 1 A.M., the three returned to Henderson's residence. At 4 A.M., friends of Matt identified his shoes.

Finally, Rob said, at 7:46 A.M. on Thursday, October 8th, he and his deputies contacted Henderson, Pasley, and Price and brought them in for questioning. The investigators broke down into planned interview teams: "The idea was that officers that had had contact with these individuals in the past were going to hopefully have some kind of rapport with them." Rob and another detective talked to Henderson, who "lawyered up" pretty quickly. But Price and then Pasley broke, and at 1:25 in the afternoon, police went to the shed at Pasley's mother's residence and found Henderson's bloodstained sneakers. Later, around 4:30, armed with a warrant, they searched McKinney's house, where they found Matt's wallet and driver's license and McKinney's bloody jeans, socks, and shoes. Neither Rob nor his team had yet gone to sleep; by the time they were finished with the initial stage of the investigation, they had been up forty-two hours straight.

McKinney was released late Thursday night from Poudre Valley and immediately picked up for questioning. Friday, at 10:40 A.M., Rob began to interview him. McKinney confessed that morning. As we looked over the text of the confession, Rob pointed out the moments where McKinney began to lose track of his story. "That's why you just keep talking to them; they usually trip up." The goal is to "keep him so off track"—by changing pace, shifting abruptly from topic to topic—"that he can't focus and keep the lie going." The cockiness that Rob would come to detest in McKinney was already in evidence that morning, during the confession. When Rob asked him if Matt had ever told McKinney to stop beating him, McKinney replied nonchalantly, "Well, yeah—he was getting the shit kicked out of him." McKinney also mocked Matt's attempts at self-defense: "He tried his little swing."

While McKinney was awaiting trial, Rob told me, he spent some time between autograph sessions concocting several escape plans, including one in which he intended to take a female officer hostage. He also tried to smash one of the jail's windows. Rob thought about that, as he handled his first death penalty case in Laramie. "As a cop, you do a lot of soul-searching on death penalties. There's a lot of different views. I consider"—he pauses and then corrects his tense—"I considered myself to be conservative, although I've changed my views in a lot of ways. But I'm pro–death penalty for the simple issue of future dangerousness. I don't want that individual to have the opportunity to get out and do it again." But he was angered when, during the trial, a reporter assumed he wanted to "put McKinney down" himself, that he felt a bloodthirst for revenge. "It sincerely pissed me off. That's not my job. When you're actually sitting in the shoes, and you know that you, as a team, are actually responsible for someone else being killed, you think about it. But it wasn't too hard for me to flash back to what Matt went through. The jurors don't get to see that, the citizens don't get to see it." Rob had, and because of it he felt he knew "exactly what [McKinney's] future dangerousness would be."

A week after we met in his office, Rob took me to the crime scene. As we drove out to the fence in a Sheriff's Office suv, he stopped in midsentence by the Wal-Mart: "Here's where it began," he told me and gestured in imitation of McKinney striking Matt. We restart the conversation, but he's made his point: the drive to the fence seems unimaginably long. It's not far—no more than a mile or two—but the rutted dirt road they turned on to makes for extremely slow driving. When I say something to Rob about how long it takes, he agrees. "They were coming here to finish him." On that dirt track, it is hard to believe the defense attorneys' claims that the two killers had been drunk and high on drugs or crazed by homosexual panic. It just takes too long to get to the fence. It's a warm and gusty early April day, the sky bright, then shuttered dark, and then bright again as a front hurries clouds overhead. We crest a small rise, and the scene comes into view.

The fence itself may be the only nonfunctional fence in Wyoming, dividing nothing, corralling nothing: just a few yards of buck and rail snaking across a faint depression, the stony ground below it scraped bare of dirt in spots by water and wind. A cross of stones is laid out beneath it now, the accumulated grief of anonymous mourners. You can see the remnants of a bouquet tangled in a patch of sagebrush nearby. When DeBree first got to the fence that Wednesday evening, the scene was pristine, undisturbed. He couldn't believe it. "Southeast Wyoming is known for its wind. And we're on an exterior crime scene—in Wyoming that can go to pot pretty quick. I got down on my hands and knees; I was marking blood spatter areas because I wanted to make sure they were photographed and eventually seized. And then I saw something that really looked strange to me, almost like a caterpillar." It was a carpet fragment, clinging lightly to the hard ground. Rob thought, "This is unbelievable. Of course, I marked that. We did a positive match of that to the truck." The footprints and tire tracks were perfectly etched; Matt's watch, his student ID, and a quarter were laid out by the fence like props. All that told DeBree a pretty clear story about what had happened there, including something I'd never heard in all the reporting of the crime—that Matt had made a run for it that night. First, he had desperately "tried to stay in the truck," Rob believes. Once out, he tried to escape. "Henderson had made a statement to Chasity Pasley that she told us about, that Matt was able to break free and tried to run. And according to what we were able to see at the crime scene, we could pretty well put that together. His wristwatch was located twenty-three feet or so from where he was tied up, and I think that's essentially what he was trying to do, was just to run. He was tackled down; then he was drug over to the fence and tied by Henderson."

It's hard to stand there, looking clear back into town, the college dorms rising in the middle of your view. That night, as Henderson and McKinney drove away from Matt, left him for dead, Henderson backed the truck into the low mound perpendicular to the fence, clotting the trailer hitch with dirt and grass, the thing DeBree would remember about the truck when he looked it over, another bit of evidence that would speak their guilt. As they drove back down the dirt road, a highway patrolman saw their retreat: he had just come off duty and was standing outside his house, built close to where the road ended. He saw the truck, heard its distinctive muffler, noticed the headlights were on and the tail lights switched off. The truck was moving slow, picking its way through the ruts, nothing panicky about it. The patrolman saw all that, paid attention as a cop would, but it didn't look suspicious, and he went inside—it was 12:30, the end of a late shift. That was the closest Matt would come to help, until Aaron Kreifels fell off his bike eighteen hours later, stood up in frustration, and saw something he couldn't fathom.

"I have never worked a homicide with this much evidence," Rob says, all these months later a bit of wonder still bleeding into his voice. "It was like a case of God giving it to us. I'm not kidding. The whole way that it broke down from the beginning to the end—it was like, here it is, boys: work it. It's almost like it pissed off God, and he says, oh well, come here, let me walk you over here, walk you over there, pick up all this, pick up all that. It was just a gift."

That initial investigation and the arrests that followed were simply "the kickoff," Rob told me. "That's when the work really begins, and once you announce the death penalty intention, it's automatically doubled—your workload is doubled. You have to prove the case, and then you've got to prove why this individual should receive the ultimate in punishment. You've got to prove future dangerousness, the viciousness of the crime, criminal history. I think I had about four or five days off through that entire year, never back to back. I was here on the weekends. That was a year from hell, believe me."

Rob is so stoic in appearance, speaks so completely in the objective language, declarative phrasing, and passive voice of police reports and evidentiary documents, that the first time he told me how upsetting the case was, I didn't think I had heard him right. But that was my mistake. Rob's general notion "of being a cop is that if you get to the point where it doesn't affect you, get out. And I think if you do take it a little bit personal, you're a little bit more motivated to get the job done, get it done right." But Rob was especially troubled, and transformed, by his work on Matt's murder: "there's so much that bothers you, and there's so many emotional ties to it." On Sunday, October 11th, a few hours before Matt died, Rob traveled to Poudre Valley Hospital. He met Judy and Dennis Shepard, who became close friends in the coming months (he tells me they're "courageous beyond words" and "so Wyoming—so down-home and lovable"). Then he went into Matt's hospital room and sat with him for a half hour. The homicide investigator held the hand of a murder victim not yet dead. It still seems to haunt him, a year and a half later. "I had some tears that night for this kid. . . . There was a lot of emotion that went with it. I didn't know Matthew, but seeing him, sitting there, when I first viewed him. . . . It was something I'll never forget."

Those weeks in October were exhausting. Before the department set up special press liaisons, Rob spent an hour and a half each day just returning phone messages from reporters. He got other calls too. "We received a lot of calls from what I would consider to be powerful voices—the governor, the White House." It didn't cow Rob much: "I even told the governor of Wyoming: 'I can only tell you so much. I'm not going to tell you anything different than I just told the media.' He's nothing to me. I don't answer to the governor of Wyoming." Not all the contacts that fall were quite so tendentious. While the department did receive some "self-important" letters and calls telling them "you better do your job right," they also received missives of support from Wyoming residents and people who had vacationed in Laramie and loved the place. And they also heard from investigators who could relate. The L.A. District Attorney's Office called to offer advice gleaned from the O. J. Simpson trial, and Rob would grow close to officers investigating the murder of James Byrd and the Columbine massacre, exchanging advice and commiseration.

As the year wore on, the emotional intensity wouldn't let up; he rode "a lot of roller coasters during the trial and before that. One day you might feel you're really victorious in a motion hearing about something, then you get tested on a couple other things, and you're feeling kind of down. Then you're questioning yourself about the death penalty. . . . It was just continuous." Rob wasn't alone: "There were a lot of tears in this case, among the officers; and that was good to see, it was good to cry. We took it personal." When McKinney's trial finally ended, "we were just wiped out. It took me at least a month, month and a half, just to recover from the case." The trial had taken a toll on the Sheriff's Office as well: the investigations and legal proceedings had cost the county more than $150,000, and Sheriff Jim Pond had to lay off four deputies as a result. To Rob, that sacrifice "should show a little bit of our integrity—we're not going to back off."

Bob Beck told me that DeBree is "about the most honorable guy" he knows, and while that might sound like hyperbole, Rob's commitment to his work is unimpeachable, as far as I can tell. And it led him to a deep transformation. "There were quite a few things that affected me emotionally—the viciousness of the crime, how small he was, things to that effect. [But] I think the thing that affected me the most was actually seeing the fear in the gay community." That fear stunned him. "How can I have these people in my community so scared? My job is to protect people. If they can't be American citizens no matter what they do—that's not right." Rob spent hours interviewing gay and lesbian friends of Matt as he labored to trace Matt's movements on the night of the attack and to know Matt better. "I think that really opened my eyes—what do I stand for? I stand to protect these people, and they're scared."

"In retrospect," Rob says to me, his professional syntax working overtime, "there was a lot of growing that probably occurred with me individually. And I think I've seen it a lot with our officers. I've noticed that the joking, that we considered to be okay at the time, is not okay anymore. It's just not acceptable; it's not acceptable around me." Rob doesn't pretty up his former attitudes. "I wasn't used to being around gays," he acknowledges, and "I'll be the first to admit that I was probably involved in those types of things" (anti-gay jokes and the like). "Now that I've become more educated—I hope—there is the feeling that there's no difference." His voice is solemn. "I've come around. I've come all around now. It was stupid." When we talk again a week or so later, Rob laughs a bit at himself: he can't believe, he says, it took him all this time "to grow up."

Rob's deepening acceptance of, and affection for, the gay people he encountered in the course of his work also got him unexpectedly involved in politics. "Once we delved into the investigation, we found out a lot more, and there was little to no doubt in our minds that this was what could be clarified as a hate crime—although unfortunately under federal statutes it's not considered to be one." Sexual orientation was not among the categories protected by the federal law. "Wyoming doesn't consider it [one either]; some other states have taken the lead on it and have put it in their statutes, but we haven't."

In the year after Matt's death, Rob found himself pulled deeply into the national debate over the federal statute. He, Sheriff Pond, and Laramie police detective Dave O'Malley traveled to Washington, D.C., with the Shepards, at the invitation of the Human Rights Campaign. Arguing for a broadened statute that would include sexual orientation and grant the federal government greater latitude in the prosecution of hate crimes, the group testified before the United States Senate in closed chambers.

Rob says, "I had a blast." He met with Janet Reno—"a neat, neat lady"—and the White House chief of staff. A lifelong conservative Republican, he was surprised to find himself on the Democratic side of things. Mainly though, he liked working with the HRC—"They're just really down to earth." While the lobbying effort failed, Rob, when I talked to him in the spring of 2000, didn't plan to give up. He and the HRC were considering another D.C. trip to "take another stab at it."

Rob's argument in favor of hate crimes legislation is straightforward. Gay individuals "have a right to it." Those who would argue that the protected categories listed in the legislation somehow work counter to the Fourteenth Amendment's guarantee of equal protection just don't get it. "It's not equal protection right now, as it sits. I don't even want to hear that argument anymore." If everyone is equally protected, why did we pass hate crimes legislation for anyone else, he asks? He speaks with a measured, pointed emphasis: "If that was the truth, then why did we have to do this for the blacks? Because there was a good reason to do it for the blacks. Why did we have to do it for religion—because there was a good reason. There are people who are targeting people for who they are, what they believe in—and it's not right. I wish the government would just wake up to that fact. We're supposed to be growing as a nation, and we haven't." Rob has little patience for the religious denunciations of homosexuality that opponents often muster against the legislation. "People get hooked up on this religion aspect of it—well, God says this in the Bible, etc. If that's what God's gonna say, then let God deal with it—that's not our problem." What our problem is, Rob thinks, is that "this certain group, this minority, is being targeted."

"Here in Laramie," he acknowledges, "I think you get varied positions on this, including in the gay community." But the baseline, he believes, is that "yes, I would say that they"—gays and lesbians—"would feel threatened if they went to a bar and wanted to dance with each other." He's quick to point out, however, the far greater safety of Laramie compared to elsewhere. "As far as out-and-out violence, if you want to take comparative notes as to New York, or San Francisco, or Chicago, I mean it's continuous. From the beginning of the time of this case to its end, there were eight gay homicides in New York City. I think that everybody just focused on us [because supposedly] we're the western idiots, 'cause we ride horses and do this to gays for the heck of it. I took a lot of offense to that."

Rob acknowledges that his links with the HRC have caused some tension with a few acquaintances: "That's caused some problems with some people here." He understands the revulsion or ambivalence they might feel, as he felt something like it once himself. "But after getting to really be educated, really sitting down and talking to gays . . . I didn't care. I was having a good time." Rob regrets that his transformation might alienate some people he knows, but he doesn't dwell on it. "Those people that are giving us the looks are also the ones that weren't involved in the case, so they didn't get the emotional ties to it." And, in the end, Rob is the cop you want on such a case. I mention to Rob that the only "special right" the gay community seems guaranteed is harassment. He agrees: "They surely don't want the attention; they just want to be normal people. So leave them alone. If you want to be the guys that go pick on them, then you'll have to go through me."

The day we drove to the fence, Rob also drove me past the former homes of the killers, and that, it appears, is as close as I'll get to them. McKinney has his gag order, and Henderson has stayed quiet, and I've decided to honor the Shepard family's wishes and leave the both of them alone. If you want to get a sense of the two, there is however one other place to go.

The court files for Henderson and McKinney are kept on the top floor of the county courthouse. Usually the clerks will fetch the files and bring them downstairs to whomever asks for them, but one day in March the clerk asks me and Damiana, my research assistant, for a hand—I'm not sure which file I want, and there are a lot to haul. It turns out that the top floor used to be the county jail, and that's where you'll find the files on McKinney and Henderson, locked up and alone. Down the hall from the public defender's office, the clerk opens a thick metal door, and we push through it into the abandoned jail. Sunlight, softly diffused by dust, gleams dimly through the windows. We pass a pile of exercise equipment, and the clerk gestures toward the cells and solitary confinement lockups lining the south side of the building. Low filing cabinets crowd the center of the room that faces the cells. We dig out armfuls of thick, bound documents and head back downstairs.

Between the two cases, there are a few dozen files, and most are stuffed with the sea of motions filed by the attorneys as they argued over jury selection, evidence, witness lists, press leaks, and the death penalty. Thrust deep inside one is a cache of letters seized by the police while Henderson and McKinney awaited trial in the new detention center next door. Most are from Kristen to Aaron or Russell to Chasity. If the letters are remarkable for anything, it's for the banality of the heterosexual romance they depict. Henderson seems preoccupied with fending off accusations of past infidelity; Kristen signs her notes "Sexy" in sweet, loopy letters surrounded by hearts and flowers. They're addressed to "Dopey," McKinney's sad nickname (according to JoAnn Wypijewski in *Harper's*, a play on his large ears and his reputation as a drug user). The letter in which McKinney tells Henderson to lay the blame on him is here too. As he recounts the story Henderson should tell the court, McKinney wraps up Matt's ending succinctly: "His fag ass died." The letter is littered with wannabe homeboy chatter, McKinney's eager and inept impersonations of gangster flair: "What's poppin' over there," he asks his "bro," his "hommie."

Bound into the same files are the materials gathered for the victim impact statement: things chosen by the Shepards that might conjure Matt in his absence. There is the outline of a school essay on collecting political buttons; childhood photos, school award certificates, photocopied yearbook pages filled with end-of-the-year messages from classmates. A Mother's Day card signed by Matt and his brother lies in these pages; photocopies of Matt's Webelo badges; a sign Matt must have drafted and placed on his bedroom door, asking for privacy. It's the ephemera of a boyhood and the edge of adulthood, scraps and mementos that should be opportunity for nothing more than the occasional family pleasure of shared nostalgia, the trigger of pleasant, fleeting memory. Strung into the most fragile of nets, they shouldn't have had to bear the entire weight of a life. Penned in Matt's own hand, they shouldn't have to testify to his death.

CHAPTER SIX

On April 28th, 2000, I drove north from Laramie to Casper, Matt's hometown. When you take that trip you pass through Bosler first, a handful of falling-down buildings one heart attack away from a ghost town; then Rock River, population 190, the railroad looping along its western edge. Medicine Bow is up next, a few streets and a row of high-tech windmills harvesting the permanently whipped-up air. You can see the hunched back of Como Bluff in the distance, where the dinosaur bone wars played out over a hundred years ago and fossil hunters still dig up remnants of cruel past worlds. Then just beyond the Virginian Hotel, Medicine Bow's small claim to western fame, you hang a right into the Shirley Basin, and the world drops away fast.

Recently some researchers have argued that the old frontier persists in America, demographically speaking anyway. If you categorize as "frontier" counties with fewer than six people per square mile, then 77 percent of Wyoming still falls into that lonely condition, and when you're in the Shirley Basin you can hardly deny it. The road is here, of course, and the power lines and barbed wire fences running alongside it, but otherwise the signs of human habitation are few and far between, just the occasional truck and the ever-present plastic bags caught in the barbed wire, tattered and flapping in the breeze like unofficial state flags. Alone in all that, you can't help feeling like a vagrant. A friend of mine told me that, when it comes to Wyoming, "nature" isn't the social construction, people are, and as you look fifty empty miles across the flattened grass and shin-high sagebrush to Laramie Peak, you know exactly what he means. The basin spreads out around you, smooth planes tilting into snow-dusted mountain ranges, and above it you can watch three kinds of weather at once—clear sky to the north, white clusters of smooth-bellied cumulus to the east, storm clouds trailing heavy, dark udders of rain to the west. Farther north, as you draw closer to Casper, you run into sheep ranches—the spring lambs everywhere in sight in April—and red rock and water. The branches of cottonwoods, ashen and metacarpal, rise out of deep-cut riverbeds, and the landscape is stitched with willow-choked gullies. The road angles close to the North Platte River and through some hills, and then it slides you into Casper, population 46,700.

Casper is two thousand feet lower in elevation than Laramie, which means spring arrives there a few weeks earlier. By that day in April, the city's trees had begun to leaf up, and flowers were blooming near Casper College, a node in Wyoming's small network of community colleges. Matt had lived in Casper until his family moved to Saudi Arabia, and after his high school graduation in Europe, and a stint on the East Coast, Matt came back to Casper to take a few classes at the college, before moving to Denver for a break and then heading to Laramie to attend uw. A year and a half had passed since his death, and on Casper College's campus that April evening, soFAITH—a new Casper group organized to combat "the homosexual ideology"—was making its first public appearance.

SOFAITH (Society of Families Anchored in Truth and Honor)

had its roots in a controversy at Casper College. An instructor had objected to the "Safe Zone" program, the tolerance-teaching workshop that ran occasional sessions—attendance voluntary—to encourage a more supportive educational environment for LGBT students and staff (Safe Zone programs have existed on numerous college campuses since the mid-1990s). The instructor, Mike Keogh, had developed a counterworkshop and dubbed it the Anchor program. In an editorial in the Casper *Star-Tribune*, Keogh deplored the "anti-family" agenda of Safe Zone, arguing that its trainers had taught participants "to tolerate and accept the most intolerable bestial behavior," while promoting "a program designed to indoctrinate the young into the netherworld of sexual deviancy." Anchor would offer an alternative: "truth, decency, and honor," according to the title page of the program's document. SOFAITH, led by Rick Koerber, a Casper resident, had sprung up to support Keogh's project. In a full-page ad in the March 5th *Star-Tribune*, Koerber announced the formation of SOFAITH: "We are organizing a very direct campaign to promote measures in communities and educational institutions designed to maintain and strengthen the family as the fundamental unit of society." SOFAITH would work, the ad said, to take the Anchor program "to institutions across the country."

But it would begin its defense of the family at Casper College. SOFAITH had announced the April 28th presentation a few days beforehand, and I had emailed Koerber to see if I could attend the evening's program. He was polite to a fault by email, and in person, when I met him that night, he was youngish and ruddy-cheeked, dressed in khakis and a white shirt. Mike Keogh introduced himself to me as well, a soft-spoken man who told me— quite sincerely, I believe—that he hoped I might learn something from the presentation. The hourlong program—first Keogh and then Koerber—fretted over the "global anti-family movement," deemed "homophobe" an intolerant epithet, and assured the audience that SOFAITH didn't hate individuals: rather, it opposed "behaviors" and policies that might promote those behaviors. The talk was spiced up with a certain squirminess about gay sex (tell me one redeeming quality about sodomy, Koerber demanded of the assembled), and the Anchor document, selling for ten bucks a pop to cover printing costs, brandished a source list of the usual right-wing suspects, Dr. Laura and the Family Research Council prominently among them, and a sample of supposedly profamily, anti-sexual-deviant organizations, including Sex Addicts Anonymous and the intriguingly named Spatula Ministries. I sat in an auditorium with about sixty attendees, including a few elderly couples seated near me, two women chatting about the *Donny and Marie Show*, a young man in Wrangler jeans and a "Christ" T-shirt, and a loquacious, middle-aged man beside me, who felt Safe Zone had gone too far in promoting the rights of homosexuals ("I shouldn't be forced to approve of that lifestyle," he told me) and required reining in. It turned out that nearly half of the audience was there to express its dismay with SOFAITH, and the Q and A, only reluctantly agreed to by Koerber, was long and rough. One man in the audience took offense to the implication that non-Christians "have no values"; another, who identified himself as a friend of Dennis and Judy Shepard, said he couldn't imagine what the speakers meant by the "homosexual agenda." He mentioned that he himself had never been "recruited" by such an agenda, had never been propositioned by a man; a younger man in the audience retorted angrily, "Consider yourself lucky." An impassioned woman asked Koerber if he thought gays and lesbians liked to be the butt of society's jokes and dislike, when they had no choice in the matter. Before Koerber could answer, the young man in the "Christ" T-shirt jumped it, declaring that they did indeed have a choice not to be gay. The divides looked unbridgeable, and it seemed clear to me—presented with an organization that conflated simply being "out" with promoting a homosexual agenda—that SOFAITH, for all its talk against hatred, left gays and lesbians no room to breathe within its brute opposition of "decency" and "deviancy."

SOFAITH has all the rights in the world to free speech and Mike Keogh to his workshop, and while Casper College surely doesn't have to endorse a program it deems corrosive to an antidiscriminatory climate of equality, I think the school's administration made the right decision to allow Keogh to present his workshop on campus while still not granting it the same institutional approval as it gives Safe Zone. We gain nothing—especially on school grounds—by shutting down speech, as intolerable as the sentiments expressed may be to some. Ignore that speech, maybe, or shine as much light on it as possible and demonstrate—often and trenchantly—the counterarguments. If their facts are fictions, prove it. But I think the responsibility of teachers is not so much to shelter students from intolerance as to give them the tools to make up their own minds about it—and to fight it if they see fit.

In the months after the murder, I heard many argue that the anti-gay sentiments of the religious right, its rank miasma of denunciation and loathing, were in some way responsible for Matt's death. I don't discount at all one part of that argument— the notion that the force of culture can shape beliefs and actions. But the path from the religious right to the fence isn't a direct one; from what I've been able to gather, neither Henderson nor McKinney was particularly enraptured by the pronouncements of the religious right, even as they grew up in a culture echoing with its noise. My point is not to diminish the anti-gay energies of certain powerful Christian constituencies but to remember that not all homophobia is religious, nor all religious homophobias the same, nor all religious sensibilities homophobic. Nuance is not perhaps the best weapon against an organization like SoFAITH, yet, still, McKinney and Henderson are not SoFAITH. SoFAITH is not ShadowGov; ShadowGov is not Fred Phelps's Westboro Church. Phelps's group is not the Baptist church attended by Lindsey Gonzales in Laramie, where a lesbian couple attends a congregation steeped in the notion of "hate the sin, love the sinner" (and where Lindsey herself shrugs off biblical arguments against homosexuality: "That was way back, thousands of years ago that that stuff was written. . . . Did they ever think about what the world was going to be like in the year 2000?"). Lindsey's congregation is not Integrity, the Episcopalian-sponsored lesbian, gay, and straight group that, since Matt's death, has organized discussions about influential figures in gay religious history and biblical affirmations of same-sex affection. A few members of Integrity told me, in a single conversation, that Laramie Christians had stuck their collective heads in the sand after Matt's death and, a little later, described the "slow, gentle erosion" of anti-gay religious sentiment they had witnessed in town. Not even all fundamentalists can be coated with the same brush. Robert Roten, a reporter for the Laramie *Boomerang*, wrote an editorial for the paper in which he identified himself as a fundamentalist and talked about the impact of the murder on his beliefs about homosexuality. In his fundamentalism, "Christians have to make up our own minds on these matters of faith. Adrift in a sea of ideas with God and the Bible to guide us, there is no other authority we bow to. We don't have to abdicate this responsibility to any preacher, priest, or guru, not to Pat Buchanan or Jerry Falwell and not to the pope." He went on to describe his careful study, since Matt's death, of gay interpretations of the Bible. The field of engagement, in other words, is a complicated one.

The day after SOFAITH's presentation, the Wyoming Activist Gathering got under way on the same college campus. Janet de Vries—a member of Casper College's Safe Zone project—was one of the organizers, along with Marlene Hines, a friendly, husky-voiced member of the Northwest Coalition for Human Dignity, which had underwritten the event. About sixty Wyoming residents, many gay and some straight, met that weekend to network and attend workshops on LGBT youth, rapid-response activism, and white privilege; on Sunday, three members of the LGBTA, including Jim Osborn, talked to the assembled for two hours about losing Matt. I met Debbie East there, a gay-rights activist from Lander who was helping to create the diversity and hate crimes awareness program on the Wind River Reservation; and I met Mark Houser, of Safe Schools for All, UGLW members, schoolteachers, and students from Natrona County High. The morning began with a game of "activist bingo" and an announcement apologizing to any transgender attendees for the architectural insensitivity of the buildings' male and female-labeled bathrooms. It couldn't have been more different from the previous night.

Or from events happening in Washington, D.C., that same

weekend. A few thousand miles away, the Millennium March was swamping the Washington Mall, and not without controversy. An LGBT rally hatched by the Human Rights Campaign and the Universal Fellowship of Metropolitan Community Churches, the march had come under heavy fire not so much from anti-gay forces as from pro-gay ones. The opposition dubbed itself the Ad Hoc Committee for Open Process, a collection of seven hundred activists, including Bill Dobbs of Queer Watch. Bill and his comrades fiercely contended that the HRC and the UFMCC were aloof and assimilationist and had excluded grassroots gay groups and organizations representing people of color from the planning of the march; worse, they had replaced such community outreach with the luring of corporate sponsors. The march's organizers, battered by the criticism, eventually added more minority representatives to their planning board and list of speakers, and the HRC distanced itself, to a degree, from the event (the organization still raised funds from a rock concert that weekend, adding to its twenty-one-million-dollar endowment). But despite the changes, the march's goals struck its critics as exceedingly bourgeois, focused as they were, as an early press release enumerated, on the desire to marry legally, to attend "the churches of our youth," and to celebrate "our diversity as a community of family, spirituality, and equality." (A major event at the march was a mass wedding, and family areas were set up near the AIDS quilt.) Bill and his fellow protesters were disgusted too by the march's heavy emphasis on celebrity appearances, consumer opportunities, and corporate endorsements, the odor of privilege hanging over it all. A bevy of stars, including Nathan Lane, Melissa Etheridge, Ellen DeGeneres, and K. D. Lang, cavorted onstage at the "Equality Rocks" concert, vendors hawked a seemingly endless supply of trinkets, and United was the march's "official" airline. In a press release, Dobbs called the march "a marketing vehicle in search of a political purpose." The consumerist, corporate energies of the march "disempowered" certain constituencies, he argued. "You see it with labor, with leather, with people of color. . . . Who's left out of this picture?" The NGLTF and the National Black Leadership Forum found such questions troubling and rescinded their original endorsements of the march, the AFL-CIO's gay organization opposed the weekend, and many gay activists and editorialists urged people to boycott the march and instead spend the weekend at home doing local gay activist work.

March organizers like Dianne Hardy-Garcia argued back, just as fiercely, pointing out that such boycotts were symptomatic of a certain privilege too—for some folks, like gay men and lesbians in her home state of Texas, marching openly for gay rights was still something you had to do out of town. It was a good point, and the march's organizers eventually announced that profits from the march would be distributed to state and community organizations (although as of this writing, the march looked to be in the red and local groups out of luck). Still, the mirror held up by the march to its participants was often bland and blond. On Sunday, as an unending line of speakers exhorted the gathered crowd, the lesbian actress Ann Heche stepped to the mike and told the assembled that standing in front of them was better than winning the Oscar and that, having experienced the discomforts of "bad press," she understood the pain of discrimination. Despite such moments, it wasn't all Hollywood that weekend, and many of the speakers angrily tackled uncomfortable issues. A Navajo activist noted the token quality of his invitation to appear at the tail end of the Sunday rally; a black-leather-clad man reminded the crowd that the "normalizing" yearnings of the march's goals failed to remember how the drag and leather outposts of gay culture had fought hard for the sexual freedom that less outré gays and lesbians now enjoyed. And that such arguments took place on the rally's stage struck me as a sign of just how far gay rights had come in the 1990s—the movement was big enough, powerful enough, that people within it could disagree, branch off, and actually fret over the potential co-optation of a once-shunned minority by corporate interests and consumer culture. It even had a bit of room for Wyoming: Judy and Dennis Shepard were in attendance at the march, continuing their call for hate crimes legislation, and Matt's name was invoked often that weekend.

Still, the distance from the Wyoming Activist Gathering to the Millennium March seemed wide. Many of the march's critics in the Ad Hoc Committee had argued that, with most anti-gay initiatives happening at the state and local level, a national march was at best only a symbolic rejoinder to those battles; and truly, back in Wyoming, the march seemed mostly like a televised sports event, something to flip to when commercials interrupted the NBA and NHL playoffs. But a friend of mine who was at the march told me this: the speakers, the concerts, the celebrities, he said, mattered little to him. What he would remember was the moment he stepped on the metro and realized the car was packed with gay and lesbian marchers. The city, its parks and streets and subways, was for that weekend a gay and lesbian city, and he felt, on that underground ride, the exhilaration of rightful possession, the thrill of traveling from margin to middle. In its own small way, the Activist Gathering, as it drew its participants together across the state's distant rural spaces, let its attendees feel something similar, let them imagine a Wyoming whose margin of political profit and personal happiness wasn't squeezed quite so tight. And in both D.C. and Wyoming that April, Matt Shepard was still being remembered.

On the trip home from Casper that weekend, the weather was wilder—lightning sliced through the indigo sky south of Elk Mountain, and thick clouds were banked up against the Laramie range like a blanket. It looked like twilight in the middle of the day, and the bleached grass, flushed faintly with new green, seemed aglow in the fuzzed light. Four cars passed me just south of Medicine Bow, and I realized they were the first cars I'd seen in over an hour. On the ranches outside town, square hayricks overflowed with pale straw, looking like fresh loaves of bread. I drove past a scattering of new mobile homes and a few antelope herds back into town. Laramie was two days from deciding whether or not it wanted a bias crimes ordinance, the first law of its kind in Wyoming.

The notion of a city bias crimes ordinance had first been pressed just a few weeks after Matt's death. The city council had passed a resolution that October expressing "sympathy for the death of Matt Shepard" and calling on the community "to begin a healing process" and "come together to express our respect and celebration for life." A loose coalition of Laramie residents—sixty or so, one member told me—had found the resolution unsatisfying, to say the least, and a few weeks after the murder they began pushing the city council to pass an ordinance targeting bias crimes, hoping for a law that could double penalties against those convicted of bias-related offenses. They would have a long wait, replete with diminished hopes.

The council first asked the coalition to hold off on its request until after the local elections in January; the citizens agreed, spending the intervening time drafting the desired law. They came back after elections, and an enhanced-penalties ordinance did make a brief bow before the council in March 1999, but only so it could be delayed. Council member Tom Gaddis had agreed to sponsor the ordinance but wanted to hold off an actual vote until after the trials of McKinney and Henderson concluded. He'd intended to introduce the ordinance that March and then win a vote to officially postpone its consideration, but, discovering that a majority of the council wanted to kill the ordinance then and there, he had to scramble. He withdrew the introduction of the ordinance entirely and promised the coalition of Laramie residents that he'd bring it back after the trials. Bern Haggerty, a Laramie lawyer who had trained police forces around the state in bias crimes investigation, was one of the leaders of the group, as were Jeanne Hurd, a local citizen, and Jeff Lockwood, the president of the Unitarian Fellowship who had organized the second vigil held the night Matt died, the vigil that had moved Ann and others so deeply. They agreed to the postponement, and if the council had hoped the agitation would blow over in the intervening months, it would be disappointed. Bern, Jeff, Jeanne, and others came back shortly after the McKinney trial, draft in hand, ready to fight.

They would, however, have to make some profound compromises along the way. In a meeting with Tom Gaddis, a handful of ordinance supporters agreed, at his urging, to trim back the law's scope. (I was in attendance, following the ordinance for this book but also wanting to support the version agreed on that night.) Bern had drafted an ordinance that would enhance criminal penalties, require police training and collection of data, and allow for victims to sue for the recovery of expenses incurred from bias-related offenses. Gaddis argued that a law that broad and ambitious wouldn't have a chance before the council, and Jeanne Hurd and Jeff Lockwood regretfully agreed to strip the ordinance down to only a few of the proposal's original provisions: the training of police officers, the establishment of guidelines for the collection of bias crimes data, and the annual publication of a summary of that data. (Enhanced penalties wouldn't have meant all that much any-way—the ordinance would have only applied in Laramie's munic-ipal court, which handles mostly misdemeanors and has limited powers of punishment.) The new, slimmed-down ordinance made no mention of sexual orientation—or any other specific categories, for that matter; the definition of "bias crime" would be left up to the city attorney, chief of police, and city manager, and some of its supporters hoped that such lack of specificity might quiet the anti-gay arguments they feared would greet the ordinance as it came up for first reading in March.

Those arguments did indeed rear up, as soon as public com-ment began on the ordinance. At least seventy people were packed into the narrow room as the council considered the ordi-nance for the first time, and close to twenty took turns address-ing the council's members. One critic of the proposed law argued that the ordinance aggressively discriminated against Christians who "opposed sodomy"; another felt that the ordi-nance would "paint a bull's-eye" on the foreheads of straight, white men. Not all the objections revolved around the question of homosexuality—council member Bob Bell leveled a slew of charges against the ordinance, arguing that it curried rather than cured resentment and prejudice, represented merely "phase one" of a much larger plan, somehow contravened the equal protection clause of the Constitution, and pandered to folks he succinctly deemed in a later council meeting "duplistic [sic] interlopers" (Wyoming's insider/outsider rhetoric was in full swing in Laramie's city hall). Another council member, Erik Stone, wondered if we needed the ordinance at all, since the Laramie Police Department was beginning to implement bias crimes training on its own (an objection, obviously, that addressed only a portion of the ordinance).* The majority of public comment that night, however, supported the ordinance. Jeff Lockwood, good with linguistic rhythm and the occasional homey metaphor both, told the council that the proposed law "prohibits no thought, it precludes no word, it proposes no special rights, it defines no privileged class, it enhances no penalty, and it contravenes no existing law. Rather, the ordinance mandates a regular 'check-up' on the health of our citizens and our city." After more than an hour of comment, the ordinance passed on to second reading, two weeks away.

The weeks between readings saw a flurry of letters to the local paper. The arguments closely replicated the stands taken in the statewide debate the previous winter: some said all crimes were hate crimes; some feared the ordinance created special categories of victims and special rights for them; others argued the ordinance would merely ensure a deepened equality for members of the community targeted for their often-reviled differences. A few writers saw the ordinance as so watered down as to be useless and opposed it on that basis. But in particular, a heated debate about homosexuality raged in the *Boomerang*. Was homosexuality a choice? Could it be "cured," like alcoholism? Does the Bible indeed condemn homosexuality as an unquestionable sin? On a letters page usually devoted to announcements concerning 5K runs and benefit balls, Laramie was getting a thrilling earful.

The ordinance would pass second reading, after another standing-room-only debate. After the first reading, I had tracked down the opponent who spoke against the ordinance's supposed legitimizing of sodomy; I'd hoped to interview him, but he was deeply reluctant—already encountering some harassment, he said,

---

* The previous year, Bern Haggerty had helped to organize a bias crimes training session in Laramie for local law enforcement. It was canceled because of lack of participation. But the training had a fee attached, and cash-strapped local agencies probably couldn't afford to send their employees. As of this writing, Laramie's police chief had undergone such training and was preparing to offer it to his force. As Jeff Lockwood pointed out to the council, an ordinance would institutionalize such practices permanently rather than leaving them up to the individual whims of future chiefs.

because of his opposition, he felt like Laramie's "real minority" and was skittish about going on the record with me. His nervousness struck me as absolutely sincere, and I backed off; but he spoke again at second reading before the council, deploring the ordinance as a thought-control tool that would brazenly force "the homosexual agenda" on an unsuspecting Laramie. Mike, continuing to expand his activism beyond the LGBTA and the Unitarian church, spoke in support of the ordinance that night. He'd told me a few weeks before that he was ambivalent about bias crimes legislation:

> I was raised Republican and conservative, and I ultimately feel there shouldn't be a need for this. But we're in a transition period and [these laws] are the most effective way of getting to the point where we don't need this kind of stuff. My sexual orientation is nobody's business, and it shouldn't be, but I'm making it other people's business because we're in a transition period. But there will be a day when it won't be an issue. If you can do a little bit of education here, get people past that ignorance factor, and say look, I'm not messing with you, don't mess with me . . .

then the community, he felt, will grow more tolerant.

Mike used his time before the council to argue that the new law would embrace minority acquaintances of his that felt deeply alienated within the confines of Laramie. His depiction was confirmed by a young man I'd met through the city council meetings—Dave, a Mexican-American resident of Laramie, who talked to me about the frustrating constraints he'd experienced here. Dave delivers furniture for a local business; he's considering getting a degree at the university, but mainly he's thinking about going back to Chicago, where he lived before moving to Laramie in his sophomore year of high school and whose ethnic vibrancy and complexity he clearly misses deeply. Everywhere he goes in Laramie, he told me, he sees "a split, a separation" between whites and minorities, intertwined, although not in perfect mimicry, with a divide between white-collar professionals and blue-collar laborers; and he has "felt unwelcome," felt "enclosed," felt "a lack of acceptance based not on hostility but on misunderstanding" here—not a "general misunderstanding, but a misunderstanding based on ignorance." Dave's not speaking the language of self-pity; he mostly shrugs off what he sees, but sharp-eyed, funny, and restless, he still sees it nonetheless. "It's not a particularly racist town," he said of Laramie, "but you don't see a bunch of cowboys hanging out with a bunch of black athletes. It just doesn't happen." He wanted the ordinance to pass and had been following it closely. As we mulled over the politics of the proposed law, Dave cooked up an imaginary amendment: a penalty that would require bias crimes offenders to go door-to-door in their community, acknowledging their crime, kind of like the punishment often imposed on pedophiles.

After passing second reading, the ordinance hit a brief road bump when the third reading was postponed on April 18th (two of the nine council members were absent that night, and Jeff told me later that Gaddis feared the votes weren't there for passage). The final vote was held on May 2nd. It was another packed room, and as I looked around, I saw many of the people I'd spent the last year and a half talking to: Kathie Beasley, Mike, Ann, John Little of the UGLW, nine members of the LGBTA. The discussion was fascinating that night. A young man who stepped up before the city council was asked to remove his hat and revealed a long, floppy mohawk; he told the council that the ordinance would bring the spirit of the Constitution closer to Laramie. Two men of Asian-American descent spoke passionately for the ordinance, describing discriminations past and present. One spoke of his Japanese grandfather, interned during World War II, and reminded the council of the riskiness of talking about interlopers—"Everyone before you," he said, "is your constituent"; the other told the council of a Hispanic student of his, a victim of racial profiling pulled over regularly, he claimed, by the Laramie police. A white man rushed to the microphone in angry response, refusing to credit such viewpoints. Laramie, he insisted, was a "friendly place"; the minority residents he knew were "successful and well liked." Kathie Beasley took the mike near the end of the comment period. Looking at the TV cameras rather than the council—the meetings were televised on the local public access station, and a number of Laramie residents (at least ones I knew) watched them—Kathie announced WAVP's strong support of the ordinance and told the television audience, "For all of you out there who are afraid, this is just the first step toward protecting you." The last Laramie resident to speak told the council this: "I am so much a WASP that I can't even get a suntan." But she supported the ordinance. "Today is Holocaust Awareness Day," she said. "What a fitting time for us to make this decision." Then she reminded the council that if they had lost a son, they wouldn't think twice about how to vote, and sat down. The ordinance passed by the slimmest of margins, by five to four. Laramie had its bias crimes law.

It seemed to me, after the passage of the ordinance, that it was easy to criticize. From the outside, if you didn't know about the genuine and hard labor of council member Gaddis and residents like Jeff, Jeanne, and Bern, the law could look merely like a public relations move to clean up Laramie's image, a sop thrown to the media and the nation, even though it was far from it in the minds of the citizens who had spent months crafting its passage. From the inside, if you desired tougher punishments for bias crimes, the ordinance was a loser indeed (Rob DeBree told me the ordinance struck him as toothless, "feel-good fluff"). And it remains true that if the police chief wanted to, he could merely pass around a handout and call it "training." But to me, the fact that the debate had pulled people like Mike, Dave, and Kathie into the city council's chambers was valuable in itself, and the ordinance insisted on a kind of public accountability that—while it wouldn't repair the subtle social divisions Dave had described—still, in the long run, might create some new trust between Laramie's minorities and its mostly white police and politicians. And it seemed to me too that to dismiss the ordinance as a total sellout was something of a luxury, something you could do only if the bias it worked against was mostly a hypothetical in your own life. Mainly, though, I liked the process that got Laramie the ordinance, that drew such different people into the same room. That's not to romanticize small-town politics, to dreamily believe that, down here at the local level, we can all get along: clearly, some things remained terribly angry and incommensurable there in city hall. What I do mean is that, fairly quickly, theorizing the shortcomings and insufficiencies of certain political actions becomes worthless. If people stayed away from the ordinance because it didn't meet a certain standard of political purity—if they stayed away from the Millennium March, or the Wyoming Activist Gathering, or anything else for that matter— they certainly had that right. But what you could see the night the ordinance passed was how change happens in a multitude of places, through a multitude of styles. The ordinance, the march, the gathering; the Wyoming Anti-Violence Project, the angel action, the church groups; maybe even those damn celebrity concerts—change for the better was working somewhere in all of them, even as they simultaneously housed each other's critics and antagonists. What you can learn from these things, from people like Kathie and Mike, is that you get political power by acting like you have it. The fears of the ordinance's opponents—that it would give gays and lesbians "a foot in the door"—were quite right; the ordinance, like so many of the events after Matt's death, did indeed foster their movement into public life and political activism. Within limits, of course; but, still, you create power for yourself by acting like it's already in your possession—by starting an organization or standing before politicians as if they should listen to you. No one—especially if you're gay—is going to give that power to you. Here in Laramie, some people made it for themselves.

As I finished this book, I got back in touch with a few of the people I'd interviewed in the months before. Jim Osborn, still working at the university and devoting himself to the LGBTA, told me that "Laramie is a much more aware place now. You can't any longer say that you're not affected by gay issues if you live here." Chad, who'd guided me through the gay online world the previous summer, was graduating and on his way to study queer theory at New York University. His love for Wyoming was still mixed, a delicate balancing act. "The closeting in Wyoming is still a hindrance," he wrote to me one day. "I still hear comments like 'How can you find a gay man in Wyoming? Look for the wife and kids!' or 'I am sorry, I can't see you anymore. When I have kids I don't want them to know their dad's a fag.' " But Chad isn't ready to shake Wyoming off entirely. At the library, the section devoted to gay and lesbian topics is full of donated books, he told me happily (even as he described some graffiti he'd found in a library men's room: next to a come-hither note inviting a "hookup," someone had scrawled "Silly Fags—that's a good way to get lynched to a fence"). "I am proud of myself and I am proud of the way uw has helped me grow and accept myself," he wrote. "The media—they painted the wrong picture of Wyoming. I recently read an article about *The Laramie Project*"—the Tectonic Theater Project's play—"and the performers were quoted as saying that they went out in pairs to be safe." Chad couldn't believe it. "I instantly thought—What the hell? Like Wyoming is a scary place? I still don't lock my doors at night. I am sure I will have to make major adjustments in my life when I move to New York. In many ways, I see myself in New York being the naive, confused student who will have to learn to lock my doors." But that's fine with him, he wrote: "I wouldn't trade my life for anything."

Mary Jane spoke some final words to me about the university and Laramie as well, words a little less sanguine than Chad's. She added up the recent changes here:

> The university has now included sexual orientation in the nondiscrimination clause of the affirmative action statement, and President Dubois sent out an email stating that sick leave and bereavement leave do apply to same-gender domestic partners. The bias crimes ordinance for the city of Laramie has passed. I feel good about all these actions, but have they furthered the cause of gay rights in Laramie? In my opinion, no. These aren't gay rights, and I don't want gay rights. I just want the same rights enjoyed by my straight coworker down the hall.

She feels like she hasn't got those rights yet, that they're a long way off. "We still have a governor and a legislature that will not support a bias crimes bill. My partner is still fearful that she will not get tenure if her very conservative peers find out she is a lesbian. I myself am fearful that this may be as good as it gets in Laramie."

Travis, who'd moved from Laramie to Cheyenne to live with his partner Jim, spoke in his usual clear-eyed way about why, if things were any better for him, they'd become so: "I'm pleased to say I've seen remarkable new awareness, though not always acceptance; and in the absence of acceptance, at least more tolerance—if only because of a perceived need for caution, to avoid being branded a bigot." Ann had been thinking about the effect of the murder on Wyoming's straight residents too. She wrote to me that "I have thought for a long time, and seen this to be true, that when straight people defend us, other straight people give more credence to what they say than what we say in our own defense. I see a lot of support from straight people doing a lot of good in Laramie right now"—with the passage of the ordinance—"and I think gay and straight alliances are extremely important in showing the world that we're not just an isolated group." Still, Ann, thoughtful and tough, experiences a continuing struggle over how much or how little she can be out as a lesbian in Laramie and at the university. "I've realized during these last few months, when the bias crimes ordinance was before the city council, that I have too many things in my past history that make me more afraid than I used to be, Matthew being one of them. It makes me mad, but it's true. And it especially makes me mad because I've been 'out' in almost every other setting I've lived in for twenty-eight years."

Larz was still studying for his graduate degree and still thinking hard about what had happened here in Laramie. Larz had been gay-bashed in San Francisco in his early twenties, and because of it he had felt a painful kinship with Matt: "The only difference between Matt and me is that I lived. . . . If someone could have given me a pill to cure my gayness when I was Matt's age," he wrote, "I would have taken it. To be gay meant to look forward to a sad life. I only saw sad and bad things to come of it. I would have done anything to make it go away." But, he told me, "I've tired of being a victim." And he has pushed past other needs as well.

I had to discover that no amount of external success can counter internal loathing. And I've since learned that the same people that laud me with praise (I was high school valedictorian, went to Stanford, etc., etc.) are sometimes the same people that label me

as a disgusting, loathsome homosexual. The world is schizo-
phrenic in this regard. Obtaining happiness and peace of mind in
a world that full of sickness is not easy. . . . I think the miracle of
coming out is that in discovering my true self, I have discovered a
heretofore unknown well of compassion and empathy for others.

Even for Henderson and McKinney, he told me. And today, when
someone yells "fag" at Larz, he retorts (and I can picture him
doing this wearing his sweet grin, his fine hair falling over his fore-
head): "Why, thank you for noticing. At least I'm doing something right today."

Kathie Beasley is still working with Amber on WAVP. She thinks
about Matt as she does so. "I didn't know Matthew Shepard—I
couldn't tell you what his hobbies were or how tall he was," she
wrote to me. "But I can honestly say that I have grieved over his
death as though he were my friend. I was not aware of the fact
that Matthew was an activist of sorts, that he was a humanist and
wanted to make life better for people." She learned those facts
about Matt—that he had been considering a future in human
rights activism—at an LGBT conference in Fort Collins. "That
weekend I was a wreck thinking about him and myself. . . . I
couldn't help but think, Matt is dead, but I am still alive. There
are reasons for everything, and I'm not saying that his death made
me an activist. But I do carry his spirit in my back pocket now."

Myself, I still compulsively tear out columns from the local
papers: articles about the national rise in deadly anti-gay hate
crimes in 1999; about a scholarship named for Matt at Weber
State University that conservative groups have vowed to end,
arguing it "promotes sodomy," in violation of Utah state law. I
keep collecting stories: of the campus gay and lesbian film festival
single-handedly pulled off by Cathy Connelly, of the drag king
show put on by the LGBTA that raised hundreds of dollars for the
Matt Shepard Foundation. I hear rumors I can't confirm, because
I can't get the names, of a gay student who has dropped out,
harassed hard by his dorm mates; of another gay man assaulted in
town since the murder. But mainly what I feel is curiosity about
Laramie, as the story rolls on, past the stretch recorded here into

maybe fresh territories, maybe recycled ones. When the town lost Matt, a stranger to most of its residents, it found someone to remember, and to remember turbulently, intimately, often unwillingly, and always with difficulty and disagreement. If Matt bequeathed Laramie anything, he bequeathed us the passion and necessity and freedom of dissent. And as the town continues to remember and forget, to speak the languages of tolerance and admonition both, we should all of us hold that inheritance close.

A Note on Sources

The economic statistics in Chapter Two, as well as the particulars on state bias crimes legislation, are drawn from the Wyoming state government Web site (in particular, from the divisions of economic analysis, employment, and education). The Wyoming Department of Heath provided the HIV/AIDS statistics I discuss in Chapter Three. The argument that Wyoming is still 77 percent frontier was made by Robert Lang, Deborah Popper, and Frank Popper in the *Journal of Rural Studies* 13, no. 4 (October 1997): 377–86.

In my recounting of the trials and other events surrounding the murder, I've often relied on the thorough reporting of those events by the Casper *Star-Tribune* and the Laramie *Boomerang*. I'd like to acknowledge here the energies both papers devoted to that coverage.

Acknowledgments

Wheaton College in Norton, Massachusetts, invited me in the fall of 1998 to speak about the early aftermath of the murder in Laramie. The passionate engagement of those who attended that talk was remarkable, and remembering that night helped to convince me several months later that a book like this might be worth writing. My thanks to all who came that night and especially to the gay-straight student alliance that planned the event.

Ann Miller, my editor at Columbia, offered me unlimited patience, painstaking editorial attention, and warm support. Sarah St. Onge did fantastic work on the manuscript. The anonymous readers of my proposal offered encouragement and welcome advice, and Damiana Gibbons's research assistance and good humor were both invaluable.

I'm grateful to the members of the University of Wyoming English Department for their support; in particular, Keith Hull, Peter Parolin, Susan Frye, and Janice Harris have selflessly listened to me work out—I'm sure at tedious length—ideas for the book. So have Amy Tigner, Cathy Connelly, and Zackie Salmon—thanks to all three for their friendship and penetrating insight. The women's studies program invited me to present early results of my research at a brown-bag talk, a lively occasion—I'm grateful to everyone who attended. And I've learned much about Wyoming from my terrific students at the university.

I've been fortunate to meet some wonderful artists and activists who have been drawn to Laramie to explore and depict what has happened here. Filmmaker Bev Seckinger has been an enlivening presence every time she has come to town. I've missed Adam Mastoon ever since his visit to Laramie in October 1999 and am grateful to him for his photographic talents. Bill Dobbs has been a bracing source of information and political edge. My conversations with the members of the Tectonic Theater Project, especially Leigh Fondakowski, have been truly valuable to me, as we have all felt our way through the complexities of representing Laramie.

Virginia Warfield provided information via email and a fortuitously timed camping trip. Thanks as well to my lawyer, the folks at Coal Creek Coffee (where I did many of my interviews), and Mailboxes Etc. in Laramie, whose employees, even after my tenth visit, never blinked when I couldn't quite remember how to fill out a Fed Ex form.

I cannot quite capture how intensely grateful I am to everyone who spoke to me for this project. Not everyone I interviewed or spoke to has ended up as part of the final draft, but whether they have or not, I have been enlightened by the openness, generosity, and intelligence of each person who has given me time and insight. In addition to those named above, my warmest thanks to Carina Evans, Kathie Marie Beasley, Val Pexton, Bob Beck, Mike Massie, Tom Throop, Lyn Lyles, Jim Osborn, Renné, Stephanie, Lisa, Phil, Mike, Mary Jane, Travis, Jim, Ann, Janet de Vries, Mark Houser, Bern Haggerty, Peggy Hutchings, Lyn Griebel, Nicki Elder, Hauva Manookin, Meesha Fenimoore, Priscilla, Chad, Larz, Mark, Bill Smith, Jan Leonhardt, Doug McBurney, David, Royce, Jay, Robin,

Heidi, Terri DeRoon, Lindsey Gonzales, John Little, C. R. Emmitt, Joe Corrigan, Richard O'Gara, Hank Coe, Pat Nagel, Ric Reverand, Jeff Lockwood, the members of Integrity, and the members of the Unitarian Universalist Church workshop on gay and lesbian issues who welcomed me to their discussion one night. Rob DeBree deserves special thanks.

I became a faculty adviser to the LGBTA shortly before Matt Shepard was killed but never had the opportunity to meet him. In his memory, I'll be donating a portion of my royalties to the LGBTA, the United Gays and Lesbians of Wyoming, the Wyoming Anti-Violence Project, and other local organizations that have offered unstinting assistance as I've sought to learn about gay and lesbian life in Wyoming. I'm especially grateful to the members of the LGBTA, who have weathered two years of grief with tenacity and grace.

This project would not have happened without the people closest to me. I'm grateful to my family—Mom, Kathy and Bob, Alan, Donna, and Zoe—for their love, well-timed visits, and willingness to believe, despite my slacker history, that I would finish this book. I kept my father's memory close as I wrote. Nick Yasinski offered unwavering support through thick and thin—I'll never forget it. Eve Oishi's wisdom and friendship have been and will always be precious to me. Finally, I cannot begin to describe how important Joe Flessa and Tripp Evans have been to me. My days would be much poorer without Tripp's affection, brilliance, and killer wit; and I can't imagine this book, or the past two years, without Joe's kindness or his fierce eye for pretension and foolishness. I'm lucky to know them both.

Beth Loffreda
Laramie
May 2000